AS I LOOK BACK

AS I LOOK BACK
MUSINGS OF A BIRDHUNTER

by Robert Braden

Safari Press Inc.
P.O. Box 3096, Long Beach, CA 90803

Braden, Robert

Second Edition

Safari Press Inc.

1999, Long Beach, California

ISBN 1-57157-151-5

Library of Congress Catalog Card Number: 98-61283

10 9 8 7 6 5 4 3 2

Readers wishing to receive the Safari Press catalog, featuring many fine books on big-game hunting, wingshooting, and sporting firearms, should write to Safari Press Inc., P.O. Box 3095, Long Beach, CA 90803, USA. Tel: (714) 894-9080 or visit our Web site at www.safaripress.com.

Table of Contents

Preface

Rancho Amigos

You might share my aversion to books and articles that recount extravagant experiences of hunters shooting something or another, somewhere or another. Perhaps we don't care much about these blustering writers, especially if their tales are manifestations of ego. It is certainly more fun to be there than to indulge oneself vicariously by reading these inflated accounts. Please write me a nasty letter if *As I Look Back* falls into this category.

I feel compelled to share events and episodes of my life whose only common thread relates to a passion for bird hunting. Maybe it's partly an attempt to answer those who question why some people are drawn to shooting. There is a growing concern for animal rights (whatever the term means) and a general uneasiness in the minds of many about the morality of hunting in any form. Perhaps there is a bit of confusion in all of our minds regarding the way we should address the natural world—the ethical role of Homo sapiens in theaters of diminishing biodiversity.

But rest assured that I make no attempt to tackle broader issues. I am simply relating my lifetime of bird hunting with a smile of satisfaction—a tranquil smile not tortured by conscience. At the beginning of my bird-hunting life, when I was fourteen, I certainly gave no thought to the possibility that I would eventually write about so many journeys afield. The ensuing fifty-three years are, however, now behind me, which must give me some license to relate the following reminiscences and reflections.

For the purpose of providing context to the individual remembrances that make up the text, this preface contains a chronological and evolutionary account of my bird-hunting life. The reader will be able to establish in his mind the breadth of experience that I have been lucky enough to obtain, and he may also see how my attitude toward shooting underwent subtle changes over time.

My entrance upon the shooting stage took place in the Panhandle of Texas, whose populace more or less took sporting guns, and the pursuit of game, as natural phenomena, totally in consonance with a young man's upbringing. Had it not been for the change of focus brought about by World War II, my exposure would likely have begun at an age younger even than fourteen. My father was deeply engrossed in defense work during the war, and shotguns did not come back upon the market until late 1945. His desire to introduce me to bird hunting was blunted by both considerations. But a 20-bore Remington Model 11 Automatic that he had placed on order in 1944 was finally delivered in the spring of 1946. The excitement of this occasion cannot be fully expressed; it was certainly a turning point in my life.

The Sunday after its arrival, we drove out to a dump on the outskirts of town, where an unlimited supply of tin cans awaited: no clay targets for us. My father threw cans while I did my best to "hit 'em on the rise"—not an easy way to enter the world of wingshooting, but what a thrill when I centered a beer can and saw it propelled through the sky. It was surprising that I seemed to have a natural aptitude, for my other athletic abilities were undistinguished. Perhaps it was motivation; perhaps it was the fact that a BB gun had been in my hands since childhood; perhaps it stemmed from the embedded lessons of baseball, my only other modest skill. For whatever reason, the concept of lead was natural for me, and I soon began to feel at home with my beloved shotgun in my hands. We had simple safety rules. It was first drilled into my head that all guns should be treated as loaded, regardless of how carefully they had been unloaded. And even more important was this cardinal rule: Never point a gun in a direction that its discharge, accidental or not, would cause damage not intended. Frankly, this latter admonition covers about 90 percent of the requirements of gun safety.

When the autumn of 1946 finally arrived, I had my first exposure to a live target, and it was the wonderfully challenging Mourning Dove. Incredibly, the very first bird fell to my gun: a passing shot at twenty yards. I was hooked for a lifetime! Never mind that my average subsequently fell off a bit; in those halcyon days, hits were remembered much more vividly than misses, however frequently the misses occurred. Sunflower fields, gravel pits, and stock tanks were as magical to me as the African veld is to a big-game hunter. Those occasions in the field also brought me much closer to my idol and ultimate role model, Wallace Braden, the father who continued to inspire me as long as he lived.

Our only limitation to this shooting partnership derived from the demands of my father's construction business, which in those years left him little time for avocations. Fortunately for me, he compensated for his own time constraints by introducing me to perhaps the finest and most experienced sportsman ever to grace the Texas Panhandle, Mr. Bill Gunn. My good fortune cannot be overstated. Mr. Gunn was one of those rare individuals who lived life with spontaneous gusto, loved every moment afield, had the time and resources to enjoy all types of hunting and fishing, and generously shared his opportunities with others, including many youngsters like me. His outward demeanor could be interpreted as gruff, yet he had a contagious laugh and an obvious joy for living. Although in awe of his stature and knowledge, I soon learned that Mr. Gunn was more than a mentor; he became a dear friend and companion, despite the disparity in our ages. His character and reputation commanded admiration from people of all walks of life; he was truly a Christian gentleman.

This relationship expanded my shooting exposure from one end of the Panhandle to the other. We perfected my emerging skills with hand-thrown clay targets and practiced wingshooting on the many domestic pigeons that frequented his property on the outskirts of town. Turkey Track Ranch near Amarillo was leased by Mr. Gunn for hunting. It was a wonderland of game: doves, quail, turkey, ducks, and deer. When he entertained business associates, I was often invited along and given the opportunity to explore parts of this large ranch by myself, sometimes walking all day in pursuit of quail, or "sneaking ducks" at the numerous lakes and stock tanks. Never mind that I was expected to clean birds for the entire group; it was a tiny price to pay for a ticket to a youngster's paradise. My debt to Bill Gunn can never be fully repaid; but each time, over the many years, that I have taken young people hunting, I think of his guiding hand and hope that he approves—even as it has brought me joy to reverse roles.

Other individuals, with somewhat "rougher edges," also shaped my early enthusiasm for the shooting world. Each year from the age of fourteen through college, my summers were spent working on highway construction jobs—this learning experience in an era long before OSHA standards, Labor Department age requirements, and vulturine trial lawyers. We proudly referred to ourselves as road hands. Some of the hard-bitten, veteran equipment operators were just as aggressive as bird hunters: No "niceties of sportsmanship" for these guys. Though abundantly proud to be asked to join them on occasion, I quickly learned what the term "meat hunter" was all about. A covey of quail on the ground represented an opportunity not to be spoiled by flushing the birds first. It was a world apart from the sportsmanlike approach of Mr. Gunn, but these road hands presented a different sort of zeal and made their own unique impression on the fabric being subconsciously woven in my mind. They loved this respite from construction work in their own rough-hewn fashion. I doubt that any would have subscribed to the merits of gun control that now ring in our ears.

These early years afield in the Panhandle were never a lay-down hand. In fact, often we struggled to take home a limit, in spite of prodigious effort expended. Small wonder that we occasionally overindulged when the chance presented itself. Walking all day to gather up six or seven doves, or a light meal of quail, requires conviction of purpose. This point is made in the hope that you will better understand the next phase of wingshooting that came my way.

After college graduation, I was employed by a consulting firm in Houston, where I was shackled with the time constraints normally encountered by a young engineer—or for that matter most anyone on the bottom rung of a career. Family obligations were also pressing, with a wife and two young children soon in the equation. At this point, I first heard about the bountiful results of White-winged Dove shooting in the state of Tamaulipas in northeastern Mexico. Here just might be an opportunity to cram a lot of shooting into an extended weekend or two, which seemed worth a try. The outcome of this initiative boggled my mind and exposed whole new vistas, good and bad.

Yes, the dove shooting exceeded anything I had ever imagined: thousands upon thousands of birds, with whatever variety of shots, or degree of difficulty, one might wish to impose upon himself. I probably killed more birds on the first two brief trips to Mexico than my previous combined total in the Panhandle over some eight years. The bad news was the outfitter, whose name I shall withhold, but who became infamous. This renegade operator was the epitome of the ugly American, breaking every conceivable code of conduct, not to mention the reasonable regulations (such as they were then) of the Mexican government. We spent as much time running from irate landowners and government officials as we did shooting doves. Yet the birds themselves were wonderful, and just as exciting as our escapes. After a very few years of these experiences, my pent-up lust for numbers was satiated, and I had no further stomach for this type of Mexico bird hunting. But the decision to look elsewhere was one of mixed emotions, for the ambiance of Tamaulipas sans problems was delightful.

About this time, unrelated events in my life increased available time for shooting. Regrettably, my marriage ended in divorce, and fortunately, a successful business career gave me more latitude for other pursuits. My principal hunting buddy during these years was Harvey Smith, whose son Link would ultimately become my son-in-law. We jointly "discovered" the fertile bird-hunting world of South Texas, extending from San Antonio south to the Rio Grande Valley and west to Eagle Pass. The Black Bear, as Harvey was called by his friends, had a fine quail lease near Dilley, Texas, and I leased a productive ranch near Eagle Pass. These opportunities had almost the same potential as northern Mexico, minus the outfitter, logistical, and bureaucratic problems. For years at these locations, we availed ourselves of some of the best quail and dove shooting to be found in the United States.

About 1963, on a typical Eagle Pass weekend, I had a chance meeting with someone who would vastly alter my future. The name Cyril Adams came up in casual conversation during lunch at our motel, and rang a bell because my older business partner, Bob Collie, had often spoken of Cyril Adams, a brilliant engineering mentor, now deceased. When I pointed this out, I was told by a mutual friend that he hadn't seemed very dead a few minutes earlier as he passed our table. Since we had a few hours to spare before we could start our afternoon dove shoot, I decided to look up this young Cyril Adams—obviously a son that had not been mentioned to me by my partner. Isn't it strange how fate and coincidence often combine to send one down a path totally unexpected?

Our meeting resulted in immediate rapport. Although he was seven years my junior, we were both civil engineers, and we both shared the same blind dedication to bird hunting. Our personalities and aptitudes were quite different, but sometimes such contrasts can produce a close relationship, as indeed it did in our case. Cyril Adams is the embodiment of patience, restraint, deliberation, competence, and relentless determination. I am enthusiastic, impatient, imaginative, curious, and lacking in practical skills. We had both tasted the forbidden fruit: bird hunting in Mexico. But Cyril, in his indomitable fashion, decided that hunting there could be accomplished without the dubious supporting services of an outfitter. It would mean overcoming substantial logistical problems, but I was game to join him. Looking back on this decision now, I am astounded at our innocence, but impressed with our fortitude. We started down a road replete with difficulties, yet rich in reward.

Our first forays into Tamaulipas involved a large measure of trial and error. Fortunately, we both had learned some Spanish, but from entirely opposite perspectives. My training had been formal, augmented by roommates in college from Mexico City and Colombia. Cyril possessed an amazing ear and intuition for the "border Spanish" that characterizes northeastern Mexico, but was grammatically abominable when attempting to speak himself. We presented a bizarre team as we traveled through the countryside seeking permission to hunt. I would strike up a casual conversation with a landowner in my best Spanish, entirely understandable to him. But the response would be rapid and confusing to my ear, so I would turn to Cyril for an interpretation. He would translate into English, whereupon I would again address the somewhat confused rancher in Spanish. Remarkably, we were successful more often than not—as to permission at least. Hunting results were another thing: sometimes superb, sometimes quite spotty.

We finally located a rancher in a good shooting area, who was amenable to the construction of an authentic camp. We rounded up a group of diverse Houston pals who shared our interest and formed a loosely organized club whose participants were willing to share in the costs involved. This motley association had all the problems one might expect, such as scheduling, intemperance, and petty arguments, but we slowly succeeded in finding birds in rewarding numbers. In the beginning, there were only modest problems of licenses, gun permits, and border crossings. As time went on, however, and bird hunting in Mexico became more popular with a wide assortment of outfitter-guided gringos, the heretofore sleepy Mexican bureaucracy awakened to the potential of profit in the form of *mordida* at the border, and by fines and other harassment that could only be avoided by cash payments in the field. We more or less dodged these issues by being nimble and by keeping our wits about us. The antics of our own club cohorts were often more perplexing.

About this time, Cyril and I stumbled upon a rare talent, an illiterate ranch foreman by the name of Rodrigo "Rigo" Tovar. He would become not only an indispensable asset, but a valued friend for the next thirty years. At first Rigo had only his Sundays free from his vaquero responsibilities, but on these occasions he joined us in our explorations of Tamaulipas and our search for dove and quail concentrations. Unlike most of the native population, who have only a superficial interest in birds, Rigo was a consummate observer of virtually everything that transpired in his world, a world confined by geographic boundaries, but limitless in ecological complexity. His practical understanding of this world never ceased to amaze me, nor did his keen native intelligence, unburdened as it was by formal education. Needless to say, we began to learn much from him, even though restrained to Sunday availability.

Finally, we decided to risk the ire of our ranch owner by asking if we could hire Rigo on a permanent basis, expecting to be refused and possibly expelled from the property. To our astonishment he readily agreed, for he rightly saw it as an opportunity for Rigo and his large family (some fourteen children) to move to Reynosa, and for his children to become educated in public schools there. From this point forward, our fortunes in Mexico took a decided turn, *arriba y adelante*. We also made the prudent decision to move our base of operations to a new ranch location, leaving the old facilities to the more recalcitrant members of our loosely knit club.

This move, however, required construction of a new, more permanent facility to house members and guests of Club de Amigos. We decided to call the building Rancho Amigos. Fortunately, one of Houston's premier architects, S. I. Morris, was a hunting buddy and was willing to assist us with a proper design. The resulting structure was a massive, reinforced-concrete, two-story frame, divided into several large, functional spaces: an upstairs, screened sleeping porch; an upstairs, indoor, winter sleeping area; a large front porch; two downstairs dining rooms (one screened and one inside); a bathroom; a reasonably large kitchen; and a vault room to store guns and cartridges—all covered by a huge, sloping, corrugated, asbestos-cement roof. It was certainly more than a camp, but less refined than the term "lodge" might call to mind.

We enjoyed unusual success at this location for many years, until the ranch owner, a somewhat overbearing old survivor of the Mexican Revolution, began to have troubles with the neighboring *ejido*, a cooperative farming area created as a product of land reform in Mexico. When the mayor of the village was murdered by a shotgun blast (presumably at the initiative of our landowner), we decided things were getting a bit too uncomfortable for Club de Amigos, so we determined to move once more. This time we bought our own quite remotely located property. Though this purchase was complex, we had the help of Adolfo Larralde, a Mexican lawyer (and corporate executive) from Monterrey, whom we had met through business connections. By purchasing our own small ranch, we would not be subject to lease renewals and other uncertainties, and we could lease adjoining ranches of almost limitless acreage for bird hunting.

Of course this meant constructing a new, grander version of Rancho Amigos, complete with refinements and a swimming pool, but built essentially along the lines of the original edifice. The logistical nightmare of accomplishing all of this at a remote location (some twenty miles from the nearest paved road and about seventy-five miles from the U.S. border) were more than formidable. Credit for success of this venture belongs almost entirely to the combined efforts of Cyril Adams and Rigo Tovar, who seemed to have an answer for every problem. By this time Club de Amigos consisted of only four members, and we three "bystanders" contributed little but money. Cyril had a model built of the new structure, so that workmen, not accustomed to refinements such as plans and specifications, could better visualize what they were building. But it was Cyril's determination and problem-solving abilities that won the day.

The new Rancho Amigos was an immediate and smashing success. Over the ensuing years of its operation, we entertained hundreds of guests, including three governors, no less than thirty major CEOs of corporate America, three English lords, brilliant doctors from Houston's Medical Center, numerous mayors and county officials, and, more importantly, lots of nice regular folk who loved to shoot—even some coonasses from Louisiana. Our taste in guests was indeed catholic. One of the great satisfactions of my life, and I know Cyril shares this view, was the opportunity to provide a unique shooting experience for so many people. In the process, I daresay we two pulled the trigger on about as many wild, nondriven birds as almost anyone active during this era of the 1960s, '70s, and '80s. We also learned volumes about human nature and what constitutes a true sportsman. But more about this subject in the text.

Lest you assume that our entire shooting experience was embodied in the *monte* (Mexico's term for thornbush) and grain fields of Tamaulipas, be assured that we were also in lively pursuit of hunting activities in Texas. After the early fall White-winged Dove season each year in Mexico, we spent a scandalous amount of time hunting duck, dove, and quail in South Texas. My close friend, Stewart Campbell, was—and is—unquestionably the most knowledgeable and successful duck hunter of the coastal marsh ever to come to terms with this challenging environment. His fastidious attention to detail, his unremitting demand for perfection, and his equipment and blinds all came together to produce remarkable results. Stewart also had a small crew of assorted individuals from all walks of life who contributed, each in his own way, to a duck hunting "operation" that almost defies description. Each of these marsh characters shared his enthusiasm for pintail, teal, and widgeon. With their airboats and sunken blinds, they combined to put lucky guests like us into concentrations of ducks that less fortunate waterfowlers can only imagine in their dreams.

We also made the happy discovery of snipe as a brilliantly demanding game bird. Our friend Jerry Derouen, and his coonass buddies in Lake Charles, exposed us to snipe in numbers far exceeding any we had been able to locate in Texas. When bird-hunting season came to a close in Texas in mid-February, back we went to Mexico for Mourning Dove and quail, which carried us each season up to the first of April, when we were forced to resort to skeet and trap until August rolled around again. Clearly, Cyril and I were deadly serious about shooting.

In 1973, we determined that we needed to explore new horizons. The opportunity presented itself in South Africa. We had helped entertain a visiting professional hunter, Tony Challis, on one of his infrequent trips to Texas to drum up clients for his big-game safaris. Tony had the unusual distinction, during this era of professional hunters at least, of having a strong liking for wingshooting. While we were in the process of exposing him to quail in southern Texas, we cooked up the idea (a bit premature for its time) of bird-hunting safaris to South Africa, and possibly to Botswana, both of which Tony knew well. He enlisted the interest and support of the South African government in such a venture, and we were invited there at a reasonable cost to sample the shooting, as a test of how Americans might fare.

Needless to say, we were fascinated by the variety and abundance of bird life, including the many fine game bird opportunities. After a glorious trip, we were not only hooked on Africa, but on dreams of what else might be available on foreign shores. We agreed to book and send Tony bird-hunting clients, and to return ourselves in the near future. We also started investigating other countries. To cover all the adventures that ensued would be to violate the covenant made at the beginning of this preface, so I will only list some of our trips during the next decade or so:

1973	South Africa
1974	Return to South Africa (Braden and Macfarlan)
1975	Colombia (duck and dove)
1975	Yugoslavia
1976	Botswana
1978	Near Aberdeen, Scotland (first exposure to the United Kingdom)

1979	Ireland (mixed bag)
1980	Hudson Bay (waterfowl)
1982	Northern India (assortment of wingshooting)
1982	Yorkshire (Red Grouse in County Durham)
1983	Argentina (duck, dove, and pigeon)
1983	Scotland (driven pheasant and Wood Pigeon)
1983	Outer Hebrides (mixed bag)
1984	Spain (partridge)
1984	Ireland (woodcock and snipe)
1985	Botswana (mixed bag)
1985	Morocco (mixed bag)
1986	Argentina (duck, dove, and pigeon)
1987	Various locations in the UK
1988	Orkneys (mixed bag)

This list by no means includes all of our UK trips or returns to various places such as the Outer Hebrides. Neither does it define those other means by which the Brits impacted our lives. During the late 1970s, we "discovered" the shooting schools in England, and about the same time had our first exposure to English shotguns. Both had enormous influence on our subsequent enjoyment of shooting. We came to know Alan Rose (West London), David Olive (school near Basingstocke), and Ken Davies (Holland and Holland) quite well, and learned from these excellent instructors (and fine shots) just how little we knew about the sophistications of wingshooting. Our clay target experience had been almost entirely skeet and trap, which, though valuable, fell far short of what could be picked up at a proper shooting ground under the tutelage of such experts as these. The addition of style to brute effort and desire produced amazing performances for both of us.

The mystical spell of owning and shooting English shotguns struck us even harder. It was an instant love affair, from which neither Cyril nor I has ever recovered. These beautifully balanced and mechanically superior shotguns greatly enhanced the pleasure of shooting for each of us, and further modified Cyril's life: He gradually changed his career from engineering to the gun trade and ultimately became a world authority on English guns.

It was a grand ride. But tragedy befell us in the winter of 1989: Cyril was stricken with large-cell lymphoma, a fast-growing cancer. His many friends were as grief-stricken as I, and it appeared for all the world that he would not survive. Amazingly, he eventually won the battle, after a disheartening series of setbacks and misfortunes that would have devastated a lesser man.

For a period of time during his lengthy recovery, I debated even continuing my shooting life, as there were too many shared experiences. Fortunately, this decision was never forced upon me, but the sobering influence of his illness did lessen my zeal for the pace of foreign travel—at least for purely shooting adventures. Another influence, much more subtle, also increasingly affected my attitude toward the natural world, and to a degree toward shooting. Starting in 1962, I had developed a corollary general interest in birds, and I soon became a dedicated bird-watcher. At first, I listed only birds I saw in Texas. As I traveled more around the country and abroad, the listing continued and my interest broadened. Ornithology, with all its fascinating ramifications, began to turn my investigations to habitat and conservation issues, and a host of other related natural history avenues.

Since retiring from business in 1988, we (my lovely wife of the past eleven years, Myra, is also a shooter and bird-watcher) have birded in sixty-five countries and have seen some 4,200 species of birds—and we are still at it. This is not to say that we have forsaken shooting, but we want to provide time for both, and I will confess that bird-watching has, along with the passing years, tempered my attitude about what constitutes sportsmanship. This transition would likely have happened regardless of ornithological pursuits. Young shooters have a natural and understandable zeal to compile nice bags, and I suppose my zeal was more pronounced than most. But as shooters mature, those things that are most important change, in shooting and in life. "Being there" ultimately becomes the highest priority for most shooters, and with it comes a genuine affection for the birds. For some shooters, this "different slant" never comes about; for others it comes quite early, perhaps because of higher sensitivity. But spare us all from those who boast of how many thousands of doves they slay in Uruguay, or how many driven pheasant fall in one drive in Hungary.

My shooting life today is essentially a return to roots in South Texas, punctuated with an occasional trip to Argentina. I do not disdain the wonderful driven shoots in Britain or Spain, and am certainly forever grateful for experiences I was privileged to enjoy. But it is quite enough at this point to watch the sun come up in Atascosa County, Texas, and shoot a few doves at dawn. The fact that my son Stewart, Myra, and friends like Cyril and Barry Allison share these joys with me makes me a very rich man. And, as I look back, I regret not a moment afield.

Dedication

This book of remembrances would be far thinner had Cyril Adams not crossed my path. It is fortunate that our respective karmas intertwined.

Cyril not only defines the sportsman in the best sense of the word, but he has taught all who know him the meaning of personal courage. He met the demon cancer and defeated it with the same steadfast determination that has characterized his entire life. For me, and for his many friends, he has been an inspiration, and a rare gift.

Oh yes, he is not a bad shot either . . . but don't tell him I said so.

Author's Note

"Common names of plants and animals are capitalized in a bewildering variety of ways, even in lists and catalogs having professional status. It is often appropriate to follow the style of an 'official list'." (*The Chicago Manual of Style*) In my writing of *As I Look Back,* I have chosen to follow the rules set by the following texts: *American Ornithological Union, Sibley and Monroe's Distribution,* and *Taxonomy of Birds of the World.* Consequently, I have adhered strictly to the rules of these references in the capitalization of accepted common bird names throughout this book, such as Mourning Dove, Northern Bobwhite, or Blue-winged Teal. For general, nonspecies specific references, however, lowercase is employed, as in dove, quail, or duck.

About the Artist

Jeff Jackson is a freelance artist and advertising consultant. Although his educational background was in fine arts, his exceptional creativity has brought him recognition and acclaim in the world of advertising—both as an art director and as a creative consultant. He is also an enthusiastic wingshot—who has *been there*.

A Good Day with Hoot

My friend Dick Merrill is a duck hunter. Lots of folks fall into this general category, but an honest appraisal would reveal that the majority are casual duck hunters, or perhaps even fair-weather duck hunters. Real enthusiasts are different, and maybe they should be called waterfowlers, the label the Brits apply to those hardy chaps who haunt tidal flats under the most damnable of circumstances. Not that Dick has masochistic tendencies—he simply loves to hunt ducks. Deep down, I've always felt that he is drawn most to the pageantry of duck hunting. How else can one explain dedication that spans the years when the limit was pitifully reduced, or occasions when the odds for reasonable success were meager at best? And pageantry is a valid motivation, for what can be more wondrous in all of the sporting world than ducks decoying at dawn? Curiously, his passion does not extend to goose hunting—a different kind of pageantry perhaps.

But Dick Merrill hasn't limited his duck hunting to one narrow vista. To my certain knowledge (as I have often joined him), he has shot Mallard in Arkansas, Cen-

tral Flyway Duck in southern Louisiana, Northern Pintail along the coastal marshes of the Texas coast, Pothole
Duck in eastern Washington, and even an assortment of
Pacific Flyway Duck at Culiacan in western Mexico. His
"heart-of-hearts favorite spot," though, is along the
Brazos River bottoms southwest of Houston, quite near
where he lived for many years.

A portion of this woodland marsh is owned by Mr. Joe
Wessendorf, a gentleman-sportsman if ever one breathed.
It is marvelous habitat. Alongside the old meanderings and
oxbows of the Brazos River, ancestral live oak trees dominate a bottomland forest with yaupon undergrowth. The
reedy marsh of low areas, punctuated with open water, is
home to more birds than one can imagine, as well as to a
bountiful, undisturbed population of alligators and their favorite prey, the non-native nutria.

Joe generously shared his property with a very few
close friends, who came to treat the privilege of shooting
there as a sort of membership in an elite club. All of the
fortunate participants not only loved hunting ducks, but
shared an almost religious devotion to the setting—and to
the central figure of this stage: Mr. Frank Hoot, or simply
Hoot, as he was known to all. How Hoot ever first connected himself with Joe Wessendorf, or with this
bottomland country, I never thought to ask, but he belonged
there in much the same manner as the live oaks. So pro-
found was his understanding of this land that it is hard to
imagine he was not born in the marsh itself. He was a
quiet, unassuming man of undistinguished appearance, but
someone whose competence, however low-key, commanded the deepest respect. To be with Hoot in this
environment was the rough equivalent of being with a
Bushman of old in the Kalahari. His knowledge of the
woods and of the marsh was encyclopedic, just as his love
of it was readily apparent—a rare man in a rare wet para-

dise. Joe Wessendorf would keep this sanctuary so long as Hoot lived, and so long as his friends went there to hunt. He no doubt considered it a monument to memories.

My exposure to the Brazos bottoms and to Hoot came even before I knew Dick Merrill, when I hunted there on a few occasions. After my very first trip, the bird-watcher in me prompted a contact with Joe Wessendorf, seeking permission to make an off-season exploration of the property, so as to catalog the incredible variety of birds. He graciously consented and told Hoot I would be calling. So it was that I came to appreciate further Hoot's remarkable talents. It is one thing to learn the names and calls of all of the ducks at this location, which included some twenty-five species. It is an incredible feat to identify also all of the heron, egret, ibis, cormorant, Anhinga, owl, and raptor, as well as the passerine, that inhabited the woods and marsh. Sometimes Hoot would stumble over a proper name, but never a vocalization or a certain knowledge of what we were seeing. His natural curiosity and perception belied his folksy, unsophisticated manner. My grandmother always said not to judge a book by its cover.

To any hunter, his outstanding ability to call ducks, identify them unerringly in flight, and read the marsh inspired awe and appreciation. Wind and weather are obvious determinants when hunting ducks at any site, and the Brazos bottoms are no exception. Hoot had an uncanny sense, seemingly instinctive, but no doubt born of experience, to respond to conditions and put his hunters in the best location on any given morning. He could then "talk to the ducks" (by individual species) as skillfully as any caller we had ever witnessed in action. Rare was the occasion when a party returned to the dock, usually around ten o'clock, without a limit of ducks.

During the fifteen years or so that Dick Merrill lived in Houston, he was a dedicated "regular" in this woodland marsh. It is well that all members of the Merrill family are fond of eating game, and that Dick's wife Grace is a willing and capable cook, for the larder was seldom lacking ducks. Even after his business career necessitated a move to New Jersey, Dick returned as often as possible during the duck season to hunt the bottoms with Hoot. It was my good fortune to join them periodically. Strangely enough, the most memorable of these rendezvous occurred just after the first part of the split season had closed, and no shotguns were involved. We had received the sad news only a few months before that Hoot's devoted wife of fifty years had died. How tragic it is when a partnership of this duration comes to an end, and how very difficult it is for the remaining spouse to adjust. We doubted, in fact, that he would be able to do so. Dick had called me from New Jersey to see if I would be interested in yet another trip to the Brazos bottoms, to see Hoot and to soak up the spectacle of the marsh without guns. What a wonderful idea! I readily concurred.

We met as usual before dawn for our ritual cup of coffee at Hoot's house, where we "layered up" and put on our waders. It was a chilly November morning with a light north breeze and not a cloud in the sky: a real bluebird day. Hoot seemed quite glad to see us, but there was an unmistakable aura of melancholy that permeated his simple home—someone, and something, definitely missing.

At the dock, Hoot cranked up his small outboard on the ancient skiff that had carried so many hunters and decoys into this enchanted marsh. Our lights picked up the yellow-white reflection of alligator eyes peering from the levee that bordered the entrance channel. Within fifteen minutes, we three sat in an accustomed blind in the pitch-black darkness of this clear autumn night. It felt good to smoke a cigar and sip coffee from a well-dented thermos. Naturally, we talked of times past, of ducks missed and ducks hit, and of friends who had shared this special place. Slowly, the pink sky in the east began to extinguish stars in this sector, and a cathedral-like hush settled on the marsh. Our conversation ceased. Precisely on schedule, the first flight of predawn teal swished by with that distinctive rush of wing beats, audible but hardy visible. We saw this group of five or six just as they silhouetted above the horizon like phantoms. Normally, this is the signal that it's almost legal shooting time, a prelude that arouses a responsive tingle in even the most veteran of duck hunters—time to slip a couple of shells into the chamber and get ready for serious business.

On this morning, however, it was more like the orchestra tuning up before the conductor takes the podium. The coots and gallinules soon started up their maniacal chorus, adding to the warm up. There followed almost immediately a sudden splash in the water not twenty feet from our blind; three Green-winged Teal had come in so quickly that we were not even warned in advance of their presence. We savored the moment by studying their antics with our binoculars, which penetrated the semidarkness better than natural vision. A Great Blue Heron presented himself against the eastern horizon, pumping slowly along with his neck pulled back in the familiar figure S and his mind on whatever herons think about—probably a fat frog. As the trees in the distance began to take shape, we could make out the profiles of a Northern Harrier on its favorite dead roosting limb and   an Anhinga hunkered down in another skeletal tree waiting for the sun to dry the dew off its wings. Only a hint of ground fog disturbed our view. Signs of the marsh were wonderfully familiar and pleasant.

But as the early light began to ooze into our swampy world, it was time to turn our attention to ducks. Another whish of wing beats, but this time we saw the flight of teal that produced this magical sound. We laughed aloud at the thought of how far behind these rockets we would have been. Does anyone actually score on these first teal, except by accident? Shortly thereafter, we had two more uninvited guests: a male and female Wood Duck. Although these shockingly handsome ducks are usually found in flooded woods later in the day, it is not unheard-of to see such a pair at first light. It brought back the painful memory of shooting a drake by accident one foggy morning some years before. I had made the deliberate promise to myself that I would never shoot a Wood Duck—they were just too beautiful—but on this oc-casion, in poor light, I confused the drake with a teal. Shame on me.

Hoot was beginning to call now and it was fascinating to see him turn small flights of Gadwall and Mallard. Four Gadwall landed less than fifteen yards from the blind, so that through binoculars we could appreciate the ultra-fine patterning on the breast and flanks of the drake. It is easy to understand why they were called Gray Duck by an ear-lier generation of duck hunters. We were also visited in a typical manner by a pair of Mottled Duck, those cautious cousins of the Mallard. They circled just out of range. We could see their silvery underwing linings as they turned away, looking almost as dark as their other relative, the Black Duck of eastern North America. Seldom do Mottled Duck fly in odd numbers, or more than in twos or fours, at least at the Brazos bottoms, and not often do they decoy on clear days such as that morning.

It was still quite early and we all knew the great spec-tacle of the blackbirds was about to begin. This phenomenon surely occurs at other marshes under similar circumstances, but I have never seen it occur so regularly elsewhere, nor with such magnitude. Rich farmlands parallel the Brazos bottoms, supporting rice production and a variety of other crops. Both stubble and weed fields, in turn, are home in winter to untold numbers of Brown-headed Cowbird, Red-winged Blackbird, Brewers Blackbird, Common Grackle, and Great-tailed Grackle (not to mention thousands of geese and Sandhill Crane). These blackbirds, by the hundreds of thousands, have the interesting habit of roosting in the marsh and adjoining forest. We were now just seeing the initial waves as they left for the day's foraging. Almost immediately, as if prompted by some signal known only to them, a great liftoff actually filled the sky with black bodies and wings, producing a sound that is almost impossible to describe, but somewhat akin to gusty gales in a big storm. The blackened sky itself seemed to pulsate to some strange beat. It was truly a spectacle of nature, inspiring awe not only in us (who had seen it repeatedly), but evidently in all birds of the marsh. Ducks flew only high above the "blackbird layer" during the brief ten to fifteen minutes that it took to unload the roost. It was as if other birds were fearful of midair collisions. Suddenly all was quiet; it seemed impossible that the sky was again clear, as if nothing happened. One minute it was Alfred Hitchcock's *The Birds*; the next instant it was over.

We always had to catch our breath after the passing of the blackbirds. But next up was a flight of about ten American Widgeon that responded nicely to Hoot's enticing whistle. They landed right in the decoys, just inside the four Gadwall that had paddled away some distance. They stayed, however, for only a few moments. Something told them things weren't right at this spot. And so the morning continued.

Around eight o'clock a lone Common Snipe winged by, angling from side to side as it searched for a proper muddy flat to investigate for marshy delicacies. I confess that my trigger finger twitched a bit at this fly-by. Dick and Hoot were obviously enjoying themselves as much as I, for we were delighted to have ducks actually landing before our eyes—quite different than when actual shooting business is the order of the day. Hoot confided to us that he had come here alone on many such occasions after the season, just to soak up the very same scene we were witnessing. Did this man love his work? Or did he just love this marsh? Fortunately for him they were one and the same.

Around half past nine, activity in the marsh was beginning to slow, prompting the reluctant decision that it was time to pack it in. Two nice items were, however, left for dessert. First, I was pleased to have a busy and vociferous little Marsh Wren drop by our blind for a look-see. He was not three feet from my eye, showing us the bright black-and-white marking of his mantle, and cocking his head as if to say, "What are you guys doing in my marsh?" Shortly after this visit, Hoot spotted a lone drake Northern Pintail winging his way high above us. An urgent whistle, perfectly executed and timed, caught his attention, causing him to turn and then decide to come in. Surely there is nothing in waterfowling more elegant than a decoying Northern Pintail. Their saber wings hook in a special way and they drop like a stone from great heights. I've seen it hundreds of times, but it never fails to stir my imagination and impress me anew. What a duck this is! When his feet struck the water, we were on our feet applauding—one round for Hoot, another for the drake. His hasty exit performance was almost as impressive as his entry.

With that finale, we cranked it up and returned to the dock—no birds to clean on this occasion. Hoot insisted we have a bite of late breakfast with him while we hashed over our near perfect day. Afterward came the somewhat awkward matter of showing our appreciation. A gratuity, however customary, had always seemed an inadequate way of saying thanks to this special man. It was particularly uncomfortable on this day, because we all sensed that it was a bonding among long-time friends. As best I remember, we left something in the kitchen in an envelope. Then came our parting thanks, and I found myself saying, "Much obliged, Frank, I hope to see you this spring when the warblers return." In all those years I had never called him Frank; he was Hoot to everyone except his wife Julie. Perhaps this memorable day tipped the scale, and I felt one degree closer to Frank Hoot.

We learned a few months later, to no one's real surprise, that he had died. We had all guessed that Julie's death would be too much for him to bear. I often think of this gentle man. We are all inclined perhaps to grade people subconsciously by their accomplishments or their contributions to society. Somehow I feel that Frank Hoot was a giant of a man by slightly different standards. His contribution was to build memories, to bring honor to his own family, and to share with us his love of the Brazos bottoms. What finer legacy could a man leave? Yes, it was a good day with Hoot indeed.

The Northern India Caper

Sometimes I think Cyril Adams reads too much. His penchant for historical accounts of bird hunting in exotic locales is particularly dangerous (though often rewarding, I must admit). These reading habits have been the stimuli for numerous bizarre expeditions to out-of-the-way places. In some instances, we have undertaken trips in an attempt to replicate wingshooting enterprises that may have taken place around the turn of the century, usually by Brits in the days of the empire. Not many people have the steadfast determination to convert dreamy visions of their imagination into the hard realities of arranging difficult journeys solely for shooting birds. Cyril is the exception.

Who else but Cyril would have put together a jaunt to Belize (then British Honduras) in the mid-1960s, or to Yugoslavia in 1975, when no Americans (that we know of) had shot there since before World War II? Who but Adams would have thought of shooting in the Outer Hebrides or Orkneys, or in Morocco of all places? Thank goodness I was able to persuade him that duck hunting on the shores of the Caspian Sea might lack even those minimal amenities we have so often had to endure. But as I look back, his crowning achievement—in terms of extravagant implausibility—was our 1982 Northern Indian Caper. It definitely fell into the category of trying to recreate shotgun sport in the days of the British raj. I should hasten to add, however, that this era ended in 1947, when India was granted its independence. We might have guessed that it is exponentially more difficult to replicate anything in such a different political climate. But, like so many of our shooting episodes, ignorance was bliss. If naiveté were a god, we would surely worship at its altar.

In the case of India, we had both been toying with the idea for several years, based on Cyril's research. We knew, for example, that birds at one time were shot from elephant back, that partridge at different locations in northern India were considered to be good sport, and that live decoys were used to call ducks in Kashmir. All of these features were appealing, but we had not a clue how we might arrange a shooting trip. Our breakthrough came through an unusual source: a Mexican friend, Adolfo Larralde (now deceased). Adolfo was a lawyer and a successful corporate executive who lived in Monterrey, Mexico, and who had gone to India some years before to hunt tigers at the twilight of the time when they could be legally taken. Three Mexican friends had joined him in this venture. Adolfo had a marvelous sense of humor, which was manifested when we inquired about the trip and asked how the hunting had gone. "Well," he said, "one Mexican got a tiger, and the next tiger got a Mexican. One Mexican died of dysentery, and I managed to survive. The score was Mexico 2, India 2." When we asked about the living conditions in India, he replied, "You gringos are always complaining about how *sucio* (dirty) things are in Mexico; compared to India, Mexico is Switzerland." This riposte said it all, as we would later learn.

But Adolfo did have one serious recommendation. He could vouch for the reliability and integrity of an Indian gentleman by the name of A. Imam, whose sobriquet was Tootoo. Although his reputation was built on hunting tigers and leopards, he was well educated and knowledgeable about all forms of sport in India. Adolfo was sure we could rely on what Tootoo might have to say about bird hunting in the north. He also had access to elephants trained to hunting. We wasted no time in sending a lengthy letter to Mr. A. Imam, explaining what we had in mind, along with a huge list of questions, mostly logistical. In due course, we received a coherent reply, complete with his proposal for being our guide and arranging all the details of our trip, including several days of shooting from elephant back. The total cost proposed was embarrassingly reasonable.

The ball was now back in our court. First of all, we had to put together our party of four shooters, and then we had to solve the one matter that Tootoo could not: shotgun shells. The sheer audacity of what we were undertaking made the first part easy. All I had to do was mention shooting from elephants and live decoys; Stewart Campbell signed on immediately. In like fashion, Cyril found it quite easy to recruit Richard Mayfield. Interestingly, Cyril and Richard had been roommates in college, as had Stewart and I, but at different schools. The problem of transporting five cases of cartridges to India was a bit more vexing. To begin with, we had zero luck with commercial airlines, who adamantly refused on the basis of policy and regulations, or so we were told. Transport by sea sounded unreliable and moved at glacial speed. Suddenly, I had the inspiration of calling our friend John Bookout, who was then president of Shell Oil Company, North America. I knew that oil companies had ways of moving equipment and parts all over the world, by air when time is an issue, which it usually is. I asked that he introduce us to whomever at Shell handled air freight. John responded in his low-key manner that he thought the problem solvable and that someone would be in touch with us. Not ten minutes later I had a call from the president of one of the major airfreight carriers, who obviously was quite anxious to see that Mr. Bookout's friends would be accommodated. It is nice to have shooting friends in high places. This company was also well informed about how to place our shipment in bonded government storage pending our arrival. The charge for all of this was negligible—thanks, I am sure, to the "Bookout connection."

We scheduled this junket for just after Christmas of 1981: 26 December through 14 January. Tootoo sent us necessary paperwork for gun permits and licenses, and we were on our way. Fortunately, we arrived in New Delhi in the middle of the night, which no doubt simplified our dealing with customs. The official on duty had never been faced with clearing shotguns, so we "talked our way through" with little difficulty, and even managed to get an official-looking seal placed on our permits. We had wisely allowed the following day to clear our shells from the government-bonded warehouse. As it turned out, our assumption that it would go slowly was optimistic, especially since we were unaware that these bureaucrats must have invented *mordida*, and then taught the Mexicans. Can you believe that one man examined each individual box, after which the shells were dutifully counted one by one by another man—never mind that they obviously came twenty-five to the box and twenty to the case? Since patience is definitely not a virtue of mine, I finally had to leave the whole matter to Cyril, whose equanimity could wear down a block of granite. Miraculously, we sprung the cartridges from bureaucratic clutches with only the payment of duty plus a small "tip." We later learned that $50 would have had us out of there in ten minutes.

After a very abbreviated amount of sightseeing—the obligatory visit to the Taj Mahal at Agra—we pressed on to Jammu in the north, for our rendezvous with Tootoo. He proved to be an accommodating, mild-mannered gentleman, whose intelligence befitted his almost professorial appearance. His normally quiet and even demeanor could be aroused to visible anger only when one subject was broached: the moratorium on tiger hunting. On these occasions (Adams often brought it up), he would produce well-worn and hideous photographs of tiger victims—or their body parts—all the while insisting that the government was committing murder by not allowing man-eaters to be hunted. I suspect his zeal might have been influenced just slightly by the corollary demise of his principal occupation. Nonetheless, he expended every effort to fulfill his obligation to us, even though bird hunting was not really his area of expertise. I give him high marks for it.

We were marginally taken aback at first exposure to his hunting "vehicle," which defies description. What can I say? It had aspects of a truck, but I feel certain that it started out as a touring car, before it was modified countless times and lost its original identity. We never learned by whom or how it was manufactured, only that it had been altered drastically by cutting torch and welding rod. We four, Tootoo, and his driver occupied the front part of this hybrid rolling stock, leaving the extended rear portion available to whatever assortment of natives (varying from no less than four to about twenty-five) might be required for our purpose. Comfort was not a consideration in any of the design modifications, nor were springs a part of the grand scheme of things.

We left for our first shooting destination on 31 December, late in the day. As darkness fell and we progressed down a roadway that made us fully appreciate our vehicle's nonexistent suspension system, the temperature dropped rapidly to freezing, then below. Suddenly, our jarring ride was interrupted by an alarming jolt that portended the loss of something rather vital to our forward locomotion. A quick inspection by Tootoo's mechanic (who, for good reason, was an integral part of the vehicle) revealed that we had broken an inner axle at the point where it connects to the wheel. The tire and wheel were "missing in action."

Things looked a little bleak, not to mention that it was pitch dark. The gringo contingent was able to produce two mini-mag lights plus one legitimate flashlight (mine). Two men were dispatched with a Mini-Mag to search for the tire in the heavy brush alongside the road, while our mechanic, Saleem, addressed the axle issue, using my flashlight to illuminate his seemingly hopeless task. With the other mini-mag, we gringos turned our attention to the important matter of surviving the freezing weather. We busied ourselves gathering anything flammable with which to build a fire. Unfortunately, most everything we could collect, without benefit of an ax, burned hot but quickly, so that most of our time was spent searching for new fuel rather than enjoying the fruits of our labors. Incidentally, Cyril was down with a raging fever that added to our concern.[1]

During the course of all this activity, which we felt sure was futile, I found myself wondering what in the name of sanity were four fairly successful American businessmen doing in a remote location in Jammu Province, India, freezing to death on New Year's Eve. At times like this, I questioned the wisdom of adventure. But, as Bear Bryant once said, "Tough times don't last. Tough people do." We had no choice but to tough it out. Our fortunes turned in about three hours. Can you believe that Saleem carried aboard a spare inner axle, which he was able to install under these trying conditions? We thought it a nice touch that the tire and wheel were finally located at just the appropriate moment in the sequence of Saleem's repair work. Tootoo remained calm throughout the entire incident, apparently inured to vehicle breakdowns. As we once again resumed our jarring progress, the thought occurred to me that I really should write Eveready, since their batteries saved the day during the lengthy repair job, but the setting might have stretched credibility.

Our first day of shooting was interesting and varied. We were introduced to three species of game birds entirely new to any of us, and to shooting conditions that were also unusual. We had been told that our principal quarry would

---

[1] *An interesting aspect of our India caper was a macabre medical experiment. The Adams-Mayfield binary, labeled the macho group, decided they would forgo any prophylactic medication, taking only reasonable care with the water. Braden-Campbell, branded the pansy group, took every precaution advised by their physicians and chlorinated every drop of water. The strategy of the pansy group took all the honors, for Cyril and Richard suffered horribly from all manner of ailments.*

be "Gray Partridge," but I seriously doubted that this bird would be the Gray Partridge (*Perdix perdix*) that is widespread in western Eurasia, despite the reference books. Our quarry turned out to be Gray Francolin (*Francolinus pondicerianus*), whose range extends from arid southeast Iran to India and Sri Lanka. We also shot two species of doves: Eurasian Collared-Dove (*Streptopelia decaocto*) and Spotted Dove (*Streptopelia chinensis*).

Brave agricultural attempts were evident in this region, even though the countryside was arid with only sparse vegetation. As most everywhere in India, population density was high, which left us wondering how so many people could survive, living on this landscape. It was impossible to escape the press of humanity, so we shot around occupied dwellings and corrals that we would ordinarily avoid. Naturally, these conditions meant that extreme caution had to be taken with every shot. Surprisingly, francolin were quite common, although we probably passed more opportunities than we took under the circumstances. Doves were rather plentiful, but we felt it wise to preserve our cartridges for more serious game.

Tootoo advised us that our elephants had arrived at a nearby community, only a few days earlier. We were astonished to learn that they had come from somewhere in the south, about 450 miles away! Our five pachyderms had begun their epic march in July of the previous summer and had reached this location only days before us, at the end of December! I expected to find them exhausted and footsore, but we later learned that elephants cannot really be hurried, because they must forage for most of the day to maintain stamina. If you ever decide to work with these beasts, I recommend you bring along your patience.

Over the next several days, we basked in the opportunity to shoot from elephant-back. It was a rare chance to engage in a mode of wingshooting that had been experienced

during the British raj. So far as we knew, our group was plow-
ing ground not tilled for decades—certainly not since WW II.
Our first learning experience was how to proceed from terra
firma alongside the elephant to a position on the howdah
placed securely on its back. We discovered that several techniques may be employed in mounting the indifferent
pachyderm. Each animal responds remarkably to the commands of his individual mahout (trainer-handler), so that it
will kneel and allow the shooter to scramble aboard, or simply permit him to step on its curled trunk—whereupon he is
first lifted and can then walk up over the head, using a grip
on its ears for balance. The howdah resembles an inverted
table, with an upturned leg at each corner; the shooter is seated
on a comfortable cushion, with his legs extended over the
front of the howdah, just on the back of the elephant's head.

Each of these elephants had been trained for tiger hunting and was steady to the sound of large-bore rifles. It was our
intention to use them for shooting Black Francolin[2] (*Francolinus
francolinus*), a species widely distributed in Asia Minor, from
Iran and Iraq to the Indian subcontinent. This particular francolin seems to prefer dense cover, as contrasted with the
agricultural habitat of the Gray Francolin. In this locale, the
cover was called (appropriately enough) elephant grass and
was not only high, but stiff and sharp, making it almost impossible to walk up birds. We formed a line with our five elephants
(four guns), spaced about twenty yards apart so that beaters
could walk between us as we progressed. Francolin generally
flushed forward, which gave us pause for concern in the beginning. The mahout rode on the elephant's head, just a foot or so
below the line of fire. We were naturally loathe to shoot over

[2] *Black Francolin are unquestionably one of the most handsome of this genus, which
includes some forty species. Males appear quite dark, having black heads and underparts,
boldly spotted white along the flanks. A prominent white cheek patch and bright cinnamon
collar add to its distinctive plumage. The patterning calls to mind the elegant Montezuma
Quail of the southwestern U. S. and Mexico.*

his head, for safety and because of noise that would be deafening, even if safe. We were quickly admonished that our shotguns were child's play compared to big-game rifles, and that we must not hesitate to take forward shots. In spite of these instructions, we found that a lifetime of safety concerns made it impossible for us to shoot directly over his head.

Even so we were surprised and pleased at the effectiveness of this program. The elephant's gait is such that we could shoot reasonably well; in fact, the biggest adjustment for me was the sitting position, not the moving platform. My colleagues particularly enjoyed an amusing episode that happened to me on one of our drives through the high grass. A local chap who was one of our beaters made the error of working too close to my elephant, and must have hit him accidentally with his stick. This activity caused temporary pandemonium. My elephant trumpeted loudly and began to spin and stomp out a circle beneath its feet. I found myself almost thrown from the howdah, but I managed to hold my gun in one hand while desperately clinging with the other arm to one of the upturned legs. The mahout brought the frightened beast under control rather quickly, but not before my "friends" had a great laugh at my rodeo performance.

Another unusual incident demonstrated how responsive these massive animals are to the mahout's commands. Stewart had observed the dexterity of an elephant's trunk, particularly its ability to grasp objects of smaller size than one would imagine. He asked if it would be possible for the elephant to pick up a downed francolin—to retrieve, so to speak. Without a moment's hesitation, the mahout replied affirmatively and then confirmed his confident answer at the next opportunity to pick up a bird. Naturally, we had to capture this moment on film since we were sure no one would believe us. Whenever I show friends this photograph, I always exaggerate. I tell my friends what a great job our elephants did of pointing birds before they flushed, with rigid trunks extended—far more effective than the average bird dog, I say, yet somehow I cannot sell this part of the story.

We learned that our elephants were effectual only for a few hours each morning, after which time they had to be allowed to forage for the remainder of the day. Our afternoons were therefore spent hunting Gray Francolin. We discovered that large livestock corrals were especially productive for francolin. They closely resembled the kraals of southern Africa and were also covered with thorny material. The difficulty came in gaining egress because of the thorns and because the gates were closed and secured with heavy rope. Our practice was to place two guns on

the outside with another one or two guns inside the corral. This enabled us to flush the birds and not miss a shot.

The livestock in the corral consisted mostly of cattle, but we occasionally encountered camels. I knew that camels were once a primary beast of burden during the many centuries that east-west trade caravans traversed northern India. Descendants of these animals are still commonly used in this arid countryside. Our knowledge of camel behavior, how-ever, was sadly lacking. We did not know that male camels experience rut and take on a disposition similar to a bull moose during this same stage.

As Cyril and I were working the inside of a corral in pursuit of francolin, a camel in rut became enraged at the sight of Cyril, who was fortunately on the opposite side from me. He attacked at a fair rate of speed, foaming at the mouth and making urgent camel noises. The unflappable Mr. Adams stood his ground (he really had no other choice) and fired one shot over the camel's head as it bore down. He saved his second shot under the assumption that blind camels have a hard time locating their target. As luck would have it, a teen-age lad was witnessing this scene and saw that either his camel or the gringo was in deep trouble. He chased after the camel with a heavy stick in hand, managing to catch up be-fore a second shot became necessary. He beat the poor brute about the head and front legs, turning him just in time. We exited this corral in as dignified a manner as the difficult ac-cess permitted, much to the amusement of Stewart and Richard, who had gained a vantage point to witness the com-motion inside. We gave camels a wider berth after this episode.

Our next undertaking in Jammu Province was totally un-expected. Tootoo took us to a dry highland area almost devoid of cover to shoot pigeons that roosted (and nested) on nearly vertical cliffs in mountainous terrain. We accessed these cliffs by an hour's climb on pathways that were worn into the rocky surface by countless thousands of Indian pedestrians over cen-turies of time. Our complaints about the strenuous hike stopped after meeting women who carried loads on their heads far ex-ceeding the weight of our gear and guns. After arriving at the cliff faces, I was quick to identify these pigeons as Rock Pigeon (*Columba livia*), true feral representatives of the pests that plague cities worldwide. It was only later when I examined photo-graphs and carefully considered the location that I realized we were actually shooting Hill Pigeon[3] (*Columba rupestris*), which superficially resemble Rock Pigeon.

The quality of the shooting was excellent, for we had many unusual angles, including birds flying below us, making it difficult to establish a line without missing above. Fortunately, Tootoo had recruited villagers to recover birds that often fell hundreds of feet below us, or came to rest on ledges that involved more of a precipitous climb than we would have dared to undertake. It was a memorable experience to add to our growing list of firsts.

Next on the program was an attempt to shoot Red Junglefowl (*Gallus gallus*) at a lowland site covered with almost impenetrable vegetation. We knew that our efforts here would not yield many birds, but we were all fascinated with the idea of shooting the feral antecedent of the world's chickens. The male of this species looks exactly like the fighting cocks of Latin America, but the female has a distinctive neck ruff quite different from its domestic cousins. Cyril managed to collect two specimens, but the rest of the group had only fleeting looks in the thick cover. Notable for all of us was the amazing spectacle of twenty-six natives, one child, and one dog loaded into the back compartment of our vehicle, in a space no larger than the interior of a minivan. This unusual day concluded our stay in Jammu Province.

Tootoo had advised us from the outset that he would place us in the hands of an experienced bird hunter when we moved north to Srinagar in the Kashmir. Our new guide was a rather sophisticated young merchant (age thirty-one) by the name of Gulam Rasool. Tootoo was entirely correct about his credentials, as we soon discovered.

Our quarters were also upgraded significantly, and we were now domiciled on a luxurious, well-appointed houseboat anchored on the shores of Lake Wular. The facade of this large boat was lavishly decorated with delicately carved

[3] *I also confirmed this identification years later in a detailed discussion with Ben King, an ornithologist who is the leading field authority on Asian birds.*

panels and moldings, making it scarcely recognizable as a houseboat. The exotic oriental furnishings within were much more elegant than anything we had seen thus far in India. It was equipped so as to be completely self-contained, including a permanent staff and chef.

These houseboats are privately owned, but are rented on occasion to domestic and foreign tourists who come to Kashmir, mainly in the summer months so they can escape the less salubrious climate in the south of India. Judging from appearances, owners are not only wealthy, but must vie with one another in the category of fanciest houseboat. Imagine a floating bordello for an oriental millionaire—missing (in our case at least) a harem befitting the appointments.

On our first day of shooting with Gulam, we were treated to an outing I will always remember for three reasons: First, it was brutally exhausting; second, the setting was spectacular; and third, it was quite different than any driven game presentation we had ever experienced. Our only indication of what was in store for us was Gulam's almost casual reference about shooting driven Chukar (*Alectoris chukar*). We had no idea about terrain or the technique of engaging these beautiful partridge.

Our very early start, hours before dawn, should have warned us that matters would not be routine. It was also soon apparent that we would be shooting in a truly mountainous region, for we could sense, even in the dark winter night, that our vehicle was climbing continuously. By the time we finally arrived at our initial destination, there was just enough light to reveal a breathtaking scene. The mighty Himalayas were in the distance, and we were surrounded by "foothills" whose base elevation was about 12,000 feet, rising easily to 15,000-foot peaks. Snow covered the ground generally, but was patchy on the slopes themselves. Since we were near (or above) treeline, vegetation was sparse amidst the rocky valleys between ridge lines. It was bitterly cold and overcast, casting a pall over the somber, yet starkly beautiful scene.

We were surprised to learn that the vehicle could progress no farther. The five of us would proceed on horseback some vaguely defined distance to a location where our beaters awaited, which turned out to be about five miles—seemingly as much vertical as horizontal. Our mounts could hardly qualify as real horses, since they were the approximate size of a Mexican burro. It was a comic scene. Our stirrups, fully extended, were a scant foot off the ground; it appeared that we weighed almost as much as our steeds. These poor beasts were sure-footed, however, and certainly breathed more easily at this altitude than the gringos they transported. Upon arrival at the rendezvous, we were amazed to encounter a gathering of about 150 local shepherds, who had been enlisted as beaters. They were in a festive frame of mind, in spite of the cold and their scruffy appearance. After receiving detailed instructions from Gulam, this small army moved off at a rapid pace until they were well out of sight. We later learned that each drive involved a two- to three-mile walk over the precipitous terrain.

Next we were told of our own assignment. For each drive it would be necessary for the five of us to climb up one of the steep, angular ridges to a position where we could form our line to intercept the path of the advancing beaters. If this task seems easy enough, bear in mind that none of us was acclimatized to such an altitude, nor were most of the group entirely fit at this point of the trip. Stewart, who is normally up to any physical challenge, was recovering from a knee injury; Cyril, at this time of his life, was suffering from dangerously high blood pressure; and Richard had fallen victim to the Indian equivalent of Montezuma's revenge: some sort of dysentery. Since my only infirmity had to do with gasping for breath under the stress of each climb, I was relegated to the next highest position on the ridge, just below Gulam, who was unaffected by the conditions. Below me were our other three gringos, who bantered constantly about whose ailment qualified him for the lower stations. Gulam later explained that Indian potentates, in an earlier time, were conveyed to their shooting positions in palanquins borne on the shoulders of servants. Good idea, it seemed to me.

The drives themselves were productive, exciting, and difficult. At great distance, we could hear the beaters shouting and jostling with one another as they avoided obstacles in their path. Coveys of Chukar were pushed ahead of the advancing line in random fashion, but they generally regrouped and flushed in packs as they flew over the guns. The topography, combined with the immensity of the mountains, made it difficult to judge distances and to focus on an individual target. Partially in our favor, however, was the extreme range that our guns had at this altitude,[4] even though we generally were choked no tighter one-quarter to one-half. As a result, we could drop birds cleanly at sixty yards, assuming that we could establish proper lead. Along with frequent misses, some truly amazing shots were made.

Another disadvantage of our position on the ridge line was the problem of taking long safe shots in front when the beaters came into range. As partridge flew up from the valley to—and over—the ridge, we would have to wait for passing shots, or take them behind. After the first drive, Gulam scolded us for being so "timid." In perfect seriousness, he admonished us to forget about the beaters and focus solely on the Chukar. We found it incredulous that so little concern would be assigned to the safety of the poor shepherds, but our host was by no means arrogant by Indian standards. It was another first for us: called on the carpet for being too safe. Naturally, we disregarded his instructions.

This arduous technique was repeated throughout the day. We would descend from our positions, mount our

---

[4] *Cyril and I knew from ballistic literature—and from actual experience at box pigeon shoots in Pachuca, Hidalgo, Mexico (around 8,000 feet)—that for each increase of a thousand feet in elevation, the standard pattern (30-inch circle at 40 yards) will pick up 2 to 3 percent more pellets. At our altitude of 13,000 to 14,000 feet, we were shooting the equivalent of extra-full chokes. Moreover, the thin air does not slow down shot as it would at sea level, so that pellets were producing significantly more energy at impact.*

horses and ride to a new ridge location. Our beaters would nonchalantly hike the required distance to start a new drive, evidently unaffected by what seemed to be agonizing effort to us. Of course, it was their briar patch. I quickly came to dread the climbs up each new ridge. I could lessen the ordeal when the next ridge to be occupied was less than a mile away. I would then retain my elevation and walk along a contour to my next position, even if it meant extra horizontal distance. At least I could in this way avoid the strenuous climb. In spite of these minor hardships, it was brilliant, memorable shooting. We completed the day exhausted, but thoroughly impressed with Gulam's competence and organizational talent, even if slightly appalled at his lack of concern for the safety of the beaters. We knew that it would be unfair to judge him harshly in this latter regard, since it was clearly a cultural issue imbedded in a caste-oriented society.

On the day following our introduction to Chukar in the Himalayan foothills, we were scheduled for a full day of duck hunting. Once again we left our houseboat well before dawn. The setting in this instance was not quite so dramatic, but had all of the ingredients of good waterfowl habitat: a large, shallow, reedy lake. We all had high expectations for an unusual shoot, since it would be our first exposure to using live decoys. The weather system that had been so threatening in the mountains on the day before had come through the Srinagar area during the night, dropping temperatures well below freezing. It was somewhat of a surprise to find that the marsh had a layer of ice about one-eighth inch thick. Fortunately, we were well equipped with waders and adequate layers of clothing for cold weather. Each of us was assigned to a small, pirogue-like boat (nonmotorized) that conveyed us to widely separated, wooden platform blinds fairly well concealed in the tall reeds. Instead of canine retrievers, each shooter was provided a local villager, whose sole job it was to pick up our ducks. We also had the services of two or three live decoys, known as callers, that were hobbled to permit feeding amongst our regular decoys. No more than a dozen decoys were employed.

It had been necessary to break thin surface ice en route to the blind. Before the decoys could be set out, the boatman and the retriever cleared away ice in front of the blind to create a sizable pond of open water. We had each been given a thermos of tea and a box lunch, with the understanding that our "pirogue" would return about midafternoon to pick us up. All of this meant that we would occupy our blinds for about seven hours or so. I was interested to note that my callers consisted of two female Mallard and one female Common Pochard (*Aythya collaris*). One would expect the familiar quacking from female Mallard, but I was unprepared for the harsh rasping croak of the Common Pochard. Its effectiveness was soon demonstrated. When a flight of ducks passed nearby, my "Judas" birds would call as if trained, turning ducks regardless of species. During the course of the day, we all enjoyed good shooting; none of us was disappointed by the performance of live decoys. Representatives of the following species were taken:

Mallard	*Anas platyrhynchos*
Eurasian Widgeon	*Anas penelope*
Common Teal	*Anas crecca crecca*
Tufted Duck	*Aythya fuligula*
Ferruginous Pochard	*Aythya nyroca*
Common Pochard	*Aythya ferina*

Ferruginous Pochard was a new bird for me, since it is rare in the western Palearctic. It is a handsome diving duck, dark cinnamon overall with white undertail coverts. The male has a prominent white eye that distinguishes it from the female. All of the other species are common to Britain.

We were now fast coming to the conclusion of our Northern India Caper, with only one day of shooting remaining. Gulam Rasool, who had certainly proved himself as a knowledgeable guide, had one more surprise in store for us: driven snipe. On this occasion, it was unnecessary to arise at such an early hour, so we enjoyed the full opulence of our houseboat. He took us to an area of cropland that had been allowed to flood partially during the winter months. There were patches of ice and snow, but unfrozen muddy areas were interspersed throughout. Once again, our competent guide had arranged for a large number of beaters. I was impressed to see that he placed our line of guns on the edge of the wetlands, with our backs to the wind—correct for driven snipe. Beaters were advancing into the wind from a considerable distance. This procedure certainly conformed to what Cyril and I had learned about shooting Common Snipe (*Gallinago gallinago*) in Louisiana— the same species, incidentally. Although it is always difficult to drive snipe, we were presented with some wonderful high passing shots, and compiled a nice bag. It was also quite a luxury to shoot snipe without the usual chore of walking through the mud.

Only one incident marred this last day. As we were walking from one driven area to the next, a snipe jumped in front of me some twenty yards out. I reacted too quickly and fired just as I sensed that there was something different about this snipe. After retrieving it, I was chagrined to see that I had shot a beautiful Greater Painted Snipe (*Rostratula benghalensis*), which is in the family Rostratulidae, only a distant cousin to Common Snipe: superficially similar, but with distinctive coloration and plumage pattern. My inconsiderate colleagues did not let me forget this unfortunate blunder.

We all had mixed feelings about our Indian bird-shooting expedition. Perhaps your travels have taken you somewhere exotic that left you ambivalent. On the one hand, I would not trade the many firsts that came our way in India; in addition, we accomplished all that we had set out to do, plus more. On the other hand, India itself was not a pleasant experience for me, and I had the distinct notion that I would never return. Why did I feel this way? The answer is complex. Perhaps I was alienated by India's sheer mass of humanity, the distressing poverty that permeates throughout, even when punctuated with spotty affluence; or perhaps I was unable to relate to a culture so foreign to the values of western civilization. I could not feel comfortable with the plight of beggars, especially children, or with the ubiquitous filth. Even in China I sensed greater optimism and energy than in India. I am sure that all of these negatives are unfair. India today seems to be arising from centuries of injustice and class orientation. I wish it well.

I must also relate three instances that made us all feel uneasy, no doubt because we four engineers could not come up with rational explanations. The following accounts are quite apart from the usual sideshow performances of snake charmers, men who walk on coals, and those who lie on beds of spikes. While in Jammu Province, we had one day of freezing rain that forced us to remain in our brutally Spartan accommodations. We passed the time reading, each of us furnished with his own brazier of live coals, our only source of heat. Sometime during the morning our coals were consumed to the point of ineffectiveness, so we called for the man whose responsibility it was to recharge our braziers from the large fire he maintained outside. In short order he entered carrying a large bucket of bright red coals. Then, to our utter amazement, he reached into the bucket with his bare hands to pick up handful after handful of burning coals to place into our four braziers. These coals were so hot that we could not place our own hands closer than a foot away. We examined his hands carefully, but they showed no special characteristics. He merely shrugged his shoulders when we questioned him.

Consider next the circumstances encountered on our duck hunt in the Kashmir. We each were provided a local villager to serve as our retriever. None of these poor wretches had warm clothing or waders, yet they stood in the freezing water for seven hours, the entire duration of our stay. Only with great effort was I able to coax my man to climb aboard the wooden blind to share some of my ample lunch, which seemed to make him nervous. He immediately returned to his position in the marsh, almost waist deep in water. The ambient temperature was obviously near freezing throughout the day. How could any human escape hypothermia under these conditions?

The final puzzle occurred on our last day of driven snipe. The hazards here were twofold. The crop had apparently been harvested by hand, which left razor-sharp, cane-like stumps about one inch in diameter, closely spaced. The ground was partially covered with slippery snow and ice, interspersed with mud. I would not have risked walking these fields with the heaviest of foot gear, yet our beaters, many of them mere youngsters, negotiated these conditions barefoot or with light sandals. I expected bloody feet at the least. There was no indication of injury or even discomfort.

Perhaps it is naive or foolish to be troubled by things we cannot understand, but I felt perplexed and even a bit shaken. Nowhere else in my travels around the world have I come across phenomena of this type. The Northern India Caper had its brilliant moments, but I shall leave further exploration to you.

Anna

An accepted adage of the sporting world is that every real shooter, over a lifetime of trials, is entitled to one great dog. Though some would say the odds are better than this, my experience suggests that one great dog per lifetime is about right. It is easy to confuse canine competence with greatness. Many shooters have enjoyed the assistance of good bird dogs or retrievers, but on much rarer occasions, we rub elbows with a superstar. Anna was such a dog.

Curiously, she did not belong to me, but then Anna belonged to no one, as you shall see. Perhaps she shared more hours afield with me than anyone else, if this indicates some ownership. Her real master was Diana, goddess of the hunt, to whom she responded in a manner not to be bestowed on any mere mortal. She lived to hunt. Her dedication left no time, no feeling, no energy for other distractions—even motherhood. But I am getting ahead of my story.

You will recall from the preface that a significant portion of my bird-shooting life was spent in northeastern

Mexico, in the state of Tamaulipas. There Cyril Adams and I carved out our little world, aided and abetted by the incomparable Rigo Tovar, our operations manager-game-keeper-local expert. In August 1976, the powerful hurricane Anna hit this region of the Mexican coast, causing extensive property damage seventy-five miles inland from the gulf. We lost our roof at Rancho Amigos, the first of several occasions that we suffered misfortune due to hurricane-related weather, including tornadoes.

As bad luck would have it, our loyal and dependable chocolate lab, Rosie, was bringing forth one of her frequent litters when the fury of the storm struck the ranch. Rosie, a fine journeyman retriever, shared the penchant of her breed as an enthusiastic and entirely catholic "copulator," when struck with the passion of estrus. In this instance, the father was a rangy blue tick hound, whose only claims to fame were an excellent nose coupled with a burning desire to track javelinas. His success at finding his quarry was evidenced by scars that covered his scrawny frame. Normally, Rosie's litters were huge, and successful considering the rigors any animal faces in rural Mexico. On this occasion, however, the storm took its toll: Only one puppy survived. Naturally, we named this hardy female Anna, in deference to the hurricane that ushered her into the world. Little did we know then that this tiny puppy's will to live would manifest itself throughout her long life.

My first recollection of Anna is of a puppy a scant five months old. It was winter, and we had put together a little family outing to hunt quail at Rancho Amigos, including my daughter, Olive, and son-in-law, Link—both experienced shots. The three of us were working Scaled Quail along a fence line punctuated with cacti that provided productive cover on that day. We were accompanied by the new puppy Anna, who had already shown great interest in exploring the area around Rancho Amigos, and who had even shown an early aptitude to retrieve—though one could scarcely call her trained. Frankly, our minds weren't on the seemingly aimless antics of so young a dog, but were focused on the frequent quail encounters.

Anna was on my side of the cactus-lined fence, out of view to Olive and Link. Suddenly the crazy puppy, only beginning to get the hang of things, tore out after some running birds. When the birds left the cover, they flushed with Anna in hot pursuit. Olive had heard my warning of quail and fired almost immediately as the birds flushed—low, as Scaled Quail are wont to do. Unfortunately, Anna ran straight into the pattern and was hit by numerous pellets. Our hearts sank when she rolled in the dust, yelping. We feared the worst, but this small bundle of chocolate struggled to her feet, albeit limping and bleeding from nose to shoulder.

Now as fate would have it, Olive had also hit a bird on this same shot; it was crippled, but headed back for the cactus. To my utter amazement, little Anna shook off her bad fortune and chased down the wounded bird, limping all the way. Credibility would be stretched if this tale included a retrieve, so I will only report that she stood steadfast until we could pick up both bird and dog. Enormously impressed by this performance, we lovingly carried her back to the truck and wrapped her in a jacket, hoping that security and warmth would prevent her from going into shock. (No vets are available in the wilds of northern Mexico.)

We left her in the care of a lad of perhaps twelve, who meant well but was not too attentive, as it turned out. We returned to the birds, as we knew there was nothing to be done for the dog. Olive was badly shaken, but the accident had been virtually unavoidable.

We had scarcely walked a hundred yards before we were again into quail. At the first flush, we downed two or three birds and were searching for them in heavy cover. Suddenly I became aware that Anna was a few steps behind me—with a dead bird in her mouth. She had jumped out of the truck window at the sound of our shots and had limped to the scene of the action. I put up my gun, cradled her in my arms, and thought to myself, *If she lives, we may have a real winner.* She did. And we did. It would not be the last time Anna proved her inherent toughness, or her desire to hunt.

As she grew from puppyhood to maturity, a process that is by necessity accelerated in Mexico, we watched the amazing transformation of this awkward-looking huntress. Most of our dogs were labs of sorts, though none would qualify for certification by the American Kennel Club. Poor Anna did not even measure up to these meager standards. She was chocolate to be sure, but there the resemblance to her mother ceased. Lanky, lean, and narrow of muzzle, she lacked any of the conformational characteristics one would expect in a lab; in fact, her aspect was truly that of a hound. The most haunting of her features were her eyes, which immediately attracted attention. To say that they were yellow does not convey the impact. They were not the yellow of a harvest moon, or the rich yellow of a sunflower, but the nightmarish pale yellow of an African lion's eyes. Pale, but intense beyond belief. They were eyes that compelled you to look at them, but then looked through you and far into the beyond. No one ever forgot Anna's eyes. And they were excellent. Fortunately, her superb vision was matched with a splendid nose and unusual intelligence.

It was immediately apparent that Anna was to be our alpha dog. By the time she was eighteen months old, she began to dominate our collection of six or seven retrievers, both male and female. Her tolerance was zero. Old dogs and puppies alike learned to bow to her matriarchal position. Woe to the dog that reached a downed bird before Anna. The dogs learned to yield to her rage on those rare instances when she was not first on the scene. Even more curious was her almost total lack of response to human attention. She never sought stroking, licked hands, or came joyously to a person's side. She was almost cold, tolerant to all but responsive to none. But what a reaction when someone picked up his gun and said, "Anna, where are the birds?" Her demeanor was then electrifying. She was always ready, always poised to hunt . . . and what a hunter she was.

Some dogs are brilliant retrievers; others are best at finding birds and working cover. Anna, almost totally untrained, was both. We could tell from her body language when she scented quail, and we followed those haunting yellow eyes when she saw doves flying above. She seemed to know instinctively when and how a bird was hit. If a White-winged Dove had only a broken wing tip and flew two hundred yards, Anna would not rest until she had run it down—gone sometimes for fifteen minutes, but almost invariably successful. With her great nose, and driven by intense desire, she would on occasion track a wounded quail as far as fifty yards. No cover was too dense, no cactus too impenetrable, no swim too lengthy.

Our dove shoots often involved ten or twelve guns of varying abilities. Anna would pass from shooter to shooter, sitting and patiently waiting for flights. She would remain faithful, however, only so long as birds were falling. How often did I hear a guest say, "I know I didn't measure up today; Anna deserted me after five minutes." She would be off to another gun.

Her retrieving feats became legends over the years. Two birds brought in at once were common. But the underlying characteristic of each tale was heart. Never did she seem to tire; never did she leave the field until the last shooter returned to the vehicles. Perhaps the highest compliment ever paid me was by Gene Hill, who shot with us often at Rancho Amigos. He said, "Braden, that dog Anna must surely be yours; no two creatures so love to hunt birds, and you are both ugly as hell." It made me proud to be compared to Anna.

Our experience with dogs in Mexico was largely a failure. We committed dozens to the test, and very few survived even the first few months. As a result of parasites, unavoidable lack of veterinary care, and rattlesnakes, life expectancy was quite poor—two or three years at the most. Our best luck was with dogs born in Mexico, but even they fell victim to the many hazards. Anna was a notable exception. She seemed immune to worms and other parasites, and had not the slightest interest in snakes, which was curious considering her overall aggression. But she did take her lumps. Her relentless pursuits meant that she covered more ground than any two other dogs, and she was confronted with accidents not of her own making.

One of my darkest moments in Mexico came when we learned from Rigo that Anna had been struck by a large piece of form lumber during construction of our second Rancho Amigos. We had arrived for a weekend; all of us were expecting to be met by Anna, whose enthusiasm derived not from personal encounters, but from the knowledge that gringos meant hunting. Sadly, Anna could hardly stand on her feet. She was bone thin and stone deaf. We later learned that she had been unconscious for three days after being hit on the head by the falling lumber. Rigo could not bring himself, by religious conviction or by affection for Anna, to perform the merciful act of ending her life, as we would probably have done under the circumstances. Miraculously, she had regained consciousness but was confused, deaf, and barely able to eat. We were all crushed to see her in this condition and could only hope that the end would come soon. After all, she was old for Mexico—probably seven years old.

We returned six weeks later and were greeted at the gate by Anna, who showed absolutely no ill effects, even to her hearing, which had returned. A vet friend of mine explained that such injuries usually involve a cranial blood clot that may, or may not, dissolve. Anna once again proved her innate toughness, and we were spared the loss of our great hunting companion.

So what kind of pups did she have? Sadly, Anna was not a mother. When we allowed her to breed, at the age of about two and a half, she produced a small litter, but showed no interest in motherhood; in fact, she ate the puppies. We were advised that this tendency would probably prevail, so we spared her the hardship of future pregnancies by having her spayed. In a way, I am glad. There could be only one Anna.

As the years rolled by and Anna became known to hundreds of our guests who came to shoot White-winged Dove, Mourning Dove, Scaled Quail, and Bobwhite Quail, she attained a status of greatness. Many times I heard over campfires at night some new feat of this unique creature. It was a source of pride to be able to say that Anna stayed with one for thirty minutes. We came to believe that she would live forever, so indestructible was her persona. Alas, it was not to be so.

By the close of her eleventh year, we knew that Anna was failing. She had naturally slowed badly, but was also losing weight and lacked the verve of old. We were torn between leaving her at Rancho Amigos and taking her to the field, for either alternative was painful for her, and difficult for us to bear. Toward the very end, I would take her by myself to a nearby stock tank where we could shoot a few doves. Weak as she was, she would trot after each downed bird and then walk slowly back to drop it at my feet. Her heart never failed, though I must confess that my own finally did. I could not watch her die. The end came peacefully in her sleep, dreaming no doubt of fresh quail scent.

It has been my great good fortune to shoot over some fine field trial pointers, and to relish the performance of magnificent retrievers, especially in Britain. But my memories of a half-breed Mexican dog named after a hurricane will burn forever. She gave new meaning to the word heart.

We thought long and hard about a fitting tribute for Anna. She was buried in a concrete vault behind the Rancho Amigos structure. One of my close shooting friends, Barry Allison, is an accomplished carver. He prepared a beautiful cross upon which we inscribed her name, her year of birth, and year of death. We added a simple tribute: *La Mejor (the best)*. In subsequent years, when I visited her grave before retiring at night, I would discuss with her the day's activities, how the birds were working, and how much everyone missed her. Funny how my eyes would tear up at the end of a long day.

A Bond of Friendship

For me there is an interesting distinction between friends and acquaintances. And in my own lexicon of terms, there is yet further differentiation between friends and true friends. Although admittedly subjective, I would define acquaintances as people I know casually, friends as individuals I know well, and true friends as that tight circle I can count on, come hell or high water. By this definition true friends are exceedingly rare. They are priceless assets in a world where we all need a rock or two to lean on when times are tough. If anyone can boast ten true friends, he is indeed wealthy, by my definition. Rodrigo "Rigo" Tovar is a true friend of mine.

It was the chance meeting of this most unusual, illiterate paisano that made it possible for Cyril and me to establish a successful bird-hunting operation in the state of Tamaulipas, Mexico. Rigo was, first of all, our local expert. He might also have been described as our operations manager—or to use the British term, our gamekeeper. Even more important, we three sustained a close bond of friendship for the thirty years or so we hunted at Rancho Amigos, and to this very day.

We first met him on a ranch located fairly near the Texas-Mexico border just south of Reynosa. The owner, who lived in town, had given us permission to build a modest camp there as a base for our shooting operations. Rigo was the resident vaquero on this property, where he lived with his ever-growing family in a rudely constructed house with thatched roof and dirt floors. It was an honest, simple existence, in keeping with the lifestyle of all other families in rural Tamaulipas during this era. We soon discovered, however, that Rigo was not a typical vaquero. His powers of observation were extraordinary, as demonstrated when he accompanied us on Sundays (his only day off) in search of shooting sites. Although his abiding interest lay in hunting local game such as javelinas, deer, and rabbits (to supplement his family's staple diet of frijoles and tortillas), he was keenly aware of every aspect of the ecology of this thornbrush country. His knowledge extended also to the game birds that were our focus, even though his only access to firepower was an ancient, rusty, single-shot, .22 caliber rifle.

Nothing seemed to escape his attention. I recall, for example, one occasion when he stopped his truck in front of my trailing vehicle and pointed to a covey of quail running through the grass alongside. I could not imagine why Rigo would stop to call my attention to such a routine occurrence. But he knew of my keen interest in birds, which prompted him to show me a most unusual phenomenon: One of the birds in this covey of Northern Bobwhite was a Northern Bobwhite-Scaled Quail hybrid. This unusual cross was apparent to me only after I scanned the covey with my binoculars (which are always at my side); Rigo had noticed it with his naked eye! His memory of the myriad roadways, tracks, fences, and property lines was also a constant source of wonderment. In all of the years we wandered through back roads of northern Tamualipas, we never saw him hesitate with respect to a proper turn or an obscure location.

It is perhaps characteristic of a highly intelligent, yet illiterate, person that he would have such an unusually reliable memory—not lulled by schooling into dependence upon maps and written instructions. For some years before he began working for us full-time, a small group of us made an annual pilgrimage farther south into Mexico to shoot a huge dove roost near Ciudad Valles. We were never able to find this site, however, without reliance upon a detailed map that showed all of the dozens of gates, turns, forks in the road, and by-passes on the way to the roosting area. The complex circuit involved at least fifteen miles of off-road effort. When Rigo initially became available to assist with the complicated logistics of transporting shotguns and shells, we realized that we would have to make a preliminary run with him so that he could familiarize himself with the route and meet the group the following morning with guns, shells, and sustenance. Rigo had never ventured before to the southern part of Tamaulipas. At the conclusion of this dry run, I foolishly became concerned that he would not be able to find the site in the dark of night, so that we could start shooting at dawn. I asked if perhaps I should accompany him, map in hand. Without the slightest hint of bravado, he shook his head no and said, *"Don Roberto, una vez es para siempre."* (One time is forever.) I did not doubt him. The following year, *he* repeated this feat, but *we* got lost. It was embarrassing when he had to come find us.

When Rigo came into our employ and was able to move his family to Reynosa, his children were able to attend public schools there, except for the eldest who was already sixteen. We were quite surprised that the opportunity for formal education was seized upon by Rigo himself, at age forty-five. As his youngsters learned to read and master rudimentary arithmetic, he joined them at home in their studies and conquered his illiteracy. We were quite taken aback when we noticed that he was sedulously reading newspapers, followed soon after with handwritten notes to us from time to time, albeit lacking a bit in legibility and grammar. Within a very few years, he was keeping books and managing a sizable Rancho Amigos bank account in McAllen, Texas. Ultimately, his native intelligence and unwavering honesty drew the attention of his neighbors in the area of Reynosa where his growing residence was located. They elected him to the city council of Reynosa (a city of perhaps 300,000 inhabitants) where he served with distinction for about ten years. As he neared voluntary retirement from politics, he was honored as the Outstanding Councilman of Reynosa for 1985, which made us all very proud.

A puzzling contradiction to his quest for knowledge was the fact that he never mastered more than a few words of English. This deficiency (if it can be called that) was of no importance, really, because both Cyril and I could communicate with him quite easily in Spanish. Some of his family learned English as a part of their schooling or employment; others followed Rigo's path and made no attempt to become bilingual. His failure to undertake this challenge was probably more cultural than anything else, for he certainly did not lack the intelligence.

Once Rigo was hired full time, we determined that it would be the cardinal rule of our Rancho Amigos operation to place him in complete charge of where and when we would shoot each day. Experience had taught us the validity of the cliché, "Too many cooks spoil the broth." Besides, we knew that his knowledge of the landscape and his understanding of the birds we pursued were vastly superior to our own. Rigo left little to chance. He regularly relied on reports from vaqueros whose judgment he trusted, and he supplemented this information by sending out his son Rigo Jr. (also our cook and ace mechanic) each day to scout areas that showed promise. If doves or quail could be produced, Rigo could be counted upon to find them and to put us in the best positions to shoot. Moreover, his powers of observation extended to assessing the shooting skills of our varied guests, and their commitment to gun safety. He unerringly placed fine shots where it would be most sporting, and positioned those not so skilled in locations less challenging. He would counsel with Cyril or me about an unsafe shooter—always a concern of ours where parties of ten guns were involved. We usually had picked up on this unsafe behavior ourselves and would coordinate plans with Rigo to separate the culprit to a safe distance, using excuses to justify a move, or, in persistent cases, a blunt explanation.

Although two years my elder, Rigo exhibited a relentless stamina under sometimes trying conditions. I remember virtually no occasions when he was idle, even when activity was not compelling. If nothing else, he always found a brushy path that cried out for clearing with his machete. Only in the evenings, when the day's work was completely done, would

I sometimes find him looking at the heavens. It pleased me then to engage him in conversation and to gain some insight into the thinking of my friend and associate. We came to appreciate his integrity as well as his intelligence. It was clear from the outset that he would require of our modest staff the same demanding standards he set for himself. For example, he would not tolerate his family drinking even a drop of anything alcoholic, as he was a teetotaler himself. His own son, Rigo Jr., was once guilty of drinking a single beer off-site of Rancho Amigos. When this transgression was discovered by his father, he was banned from the ranch for one month. Cyril and I were mortified, for fear of losing the services of such an invaluable employee. But he returned after his exile . . . and it never happened again.

Drunk gringos were another matter. Although we privately knew that Rigo strongly disapproved of drinking to excess by anyone, he never let his personal feelings be known to those of our guests who misgauged the debilitating consequences of too many margaritas. He was, in fact, tolerant of questionable conduct generally, so long as safety was not at issue. I suppose he considered it part of his job. Nonetheless, he was an excellent judge of character, and we knew full well which *norteamericanos* were his favorites. They included some impressive individuals.

On one notable occasion Rigo had to drive to Houston for some purpose now lost to my memory. We met him on the outskirts of town so we could rendezvous more easily, and so he would be spared driving in a city so foreign to him. The next day, it occurred to us that Rigo might enjoy seeing some of his dove-shooting Houston friends in their downtown offices. We visited Dan Arnold (then president of the mammoth First City National Bank), Jim Lesch (CEO of Hughes Tool Company), Jon Lindsay (County Judge of Harris County), and John Bookout (president of Shell Oil Company, N.A.). We had no advance appointments, but each of these executives altered their schedules to greet him. John even called for lunch to be served in the executive dining room on the fiftieth floor of One Shell Plaza. It occurred to Cyril and me that *this* vaquero from rural Tamaulipas had more access to these gentlemen than did we. It was born of mutual respect.

Rigo received a special invitation one year in the late 1970s from another of his gringo friends, Mr. Bill Abbey. Bill was an elderly gentleman who had often been a guest at Rancho Amigos. He was always given special attention because of his advanced age and genial good humor. Bill had observed how diligently Rigo pursued the limited number of deer still extant in northern Tamaulipas. (The pitifully thin deer population was the result of relentless night poaching by local paisanos.) He thought Rigo would love a chance to take part in a genuine West Texas deer hunt. Bill's large family ranch near Comstock, Texas, was a haven for wild turkey and white-tailed deer. Cyril, Myra, and I had shot turkey there on a previous occasion. This invitation was particularly opportune because a survey by the state had determined that some twenty doe permits should be issued to restore a proper doe/buck ratio.

We all met at the Comstock ranch for the combined deer and turkey hunt and were briefed by Bill about the territory available for hunting deer, and the location of the turkey blinds. As we rode around the ranch on the late afternoon of our arrival, we were all impressed by the amount of game, particularly does. I had no acceptable deer rifle since my gun case contains only shotguns, but a friend who had been to Rancho Amigos was happy to loan us a bolt-action .270 rifle with a nice scope. Rigo had never used a scope before, nor had he fired a rifle of greater caliber than his trusty .22. He listened patiently to our instructions, although I intuited that his mind was really on the number of deer he had just seen. Bill explained that he could kill as many does as he wished (we assumed two or three), but that any bucks were to be passed. He only had ten cartridges in his possession.

The following day before dawn, we took our places at turkey blinds; Rigo departed solo in his pickup truck for the back part of the ranch, as per his instructions. When we returned to the headquarters about ten o'clock, after successfully bagging a gobbler each, we came upon an amazing sight at the outbuilding where deer were always dressed out and turkeys picked and cleaned: Rigo had a stack of seven deer—six does and one nice buck. He was as pleased with the world as anyone could ever be, though apologetic to Bill about the buck. It seems that he simply could not resist the temptation, which, of course, amused rather than upset his host. When I inquired if he had run out of cartridges, he looked puzzled and replied, *"Hay tres aquí, todavia."* (Three are still here.) His performance was not bad: seven deer with seven shots, all shot cleanly in the neck or shoulder. He did comment that the scope was very helpful. We had to buy three huge iceboxes to pack all the nicely butchered deer for his return home. He wisely rented a freezer in McAllen to store his stockpile of venison, so that he could smuggle small quantities back across the border, thereby avoiding the avarice of any customs agent who might confiscate for himself the contents of a large icebox. No doubt this experience was as mind-boggling to Rigo's family as it was to him.

In 1987 we decided that it would be interesting for Rigo to join us on a trip to the UK so that he could better understand our descriptions of driven birds and, at the same time, see a vastly different part of the world. The idea had both merit and pitfalls. We should have known that it would not be easy. To begin with, he had no birth certificate, which was essential for acquiring a Mexican passport. Ultimately, he enlisted the support of a local priest, who attested that he had been born on a ranch in Tamaulipas. This fact was rather obvious, but we doubted that first-hand documentation was part of the process since the priest was twenty years younger than Rigo. The next issue was to arrange transportation from McAllen to Houston to London, for Rigo had never flown before and was understandably apprehensive of what might ensue. But he probably would have boarded a space shuttle if we had asked him to do so. We met his plane in Houston, of course, after the solo flight from McAllen. He was only mildly distraught. The next day, however, meant boarding a 747 for a nine-hour flight to London. He was reassured by our presence, but appalled by the size of the aircraft and the thought of so long a flight. Even the meals in flight were strange for him.

The crowning credibility blow came when Cyril explained that he would have to move his watch forward six hours to account for the time change. No doubt Rigo had enough difficulty accepting that the earth was round; the time business left him grasping for reality. Yet when we arrived at Gatwick Airport, the clocks there confirmed what he had been told. It was depressing to him. We boarded the train for Victoria Station, which went well enough until the tracks went underground, a circumstance that we had neglected to tell him about in advance. Understandably, he was a bit shaken. We had also failed to anticipate the dietary implications; poor Rigo found nothing familiar or appealing to his palate. During our two-day stay in London, he was disinclined to leave the sanctity of his hotel room and we were beginning to feel that the trip was a mistake. But we were committed to a shooting engagement in Scotland, leaving us no choice other than to press on. After assuring Rigo that this train ride would harbor no underground surprises, we left the rigors of the big city; he began to feel much better as the serene rural landscape flashed by.

The sustained cold weather was a problem for him. He was dumbfounded when he first saw horses with coverings that blanketed their backs and sides. A country so cold that even the horses needed jackets was disconcerting to a vaquero from the latitude of Tamaulipas. All of his doubts evaporated, however, when we at last arrived at the estate in Scotland where we were shooting. The gamekeeper there was a friend of ours from past shoots, and he knew in advance that we were bringing along *our* "gamekeeper" from Mexico. Rigo was welcomed as a professional of equal status. In spite of the obvious language barrier, his quick mind and powers of observation enabled him to absorb how pheasants were raised, how the large flight pens were utilized, and how the birds were managed so that they could be successfully driven over the guns. He walked side by side with the beaters, observing the skills involved in controlling the pace of the drives. He was enormously impressed. Naturally, he also viewed the results from the perspective of the shooter, standing alongside his gringo associates. By the end of the fourth day, I daresay Rigo knew more about driven pheasant than the average American shooter would ever learn.

Our return through London was less traumatic, and the flight home almost routine to our new world traveler. Rigo actually gave little indication, one way or another, about his reaction to the trip, which came as no real surprise to us. He was not the sort to display emotion lightly. A month or so later, however, I gained a better insight. In a lengthy conversation with his son Alfonso (always a favorite of mine), he confided that his father had called the whole family together upon his return to relate in detail how it was on the other side of the big water: time differences, underground train tunnels, unspeakably poor climate, and horses that wore jackets to stay warm. All in all, the journey was successful.

Despite my comment above, though, the paisanos of rural Mexico, for all their stoic demeanor, do react to emotional vicissitudes. They simply handle pain, gratitude, and even elation in a different, more dignified manner than we are wont to do in the United States. When Cyril was at one of the lower ebbs of his battle with cancer, deep into debilitating chemotherapy, he asked that I take him to Rancho Amigos for a weekend. Frankly, I think that he felt it would be his last chance to see the place and to visit with Rigo. Although I had tried desperately to reassure Rigo that Cyril would pull through, I could see doubt written on his face. We had already lost Richard Mayfield (one of the four original partners) to cancer, which had grieved us all. Moreover, Rigo had seen few cases of recovery from cancer in rural Mexico.

It didn't help matters to see Cyril in his condition at the time. He looked worse than death. The robust and hirsute Don Cyrillo, who was known to everyone in that part of Mexico, was reduced to a pathetic, enervated, and very sick man, almost devoid of hair. Nonetheless, he was greeted warmly by Rigo and our core staff. During the course of the day, paisanos throughout the countryside came by to pay their respects to their favorite gringo, many bringing small gifts. The emotion was not so much palpable on the surface as it was evident in the eyes and actions of these stalwart friends. I was forced to retire into the *monte* nearby to shed tears that lacked the dignity of Cyril's Mexican admirers. I could sense that Rigo was positively overcome with emotion, yet he maintained a warm front of good cheer. Perhaps this show of intense loyalty by so many gave Cyril that extra measure of strength to defeat his demon. I would like to think so.

After Cyril's recovery, we continued for some years to operate Rancho Amigos. Finally, a combination of circumstances that not even Rigo and Cyril could overcome—Mexican bureaucratic restrictions on gun permits, reduced concentration of doves due to changed agricultural practices, among others—made it necessary to close the book on this long chapter of our lives. It was painful for us all, but inevitable I suppose. Rigo reluctantly agreed with our assessment, and we eased the trauma slightly by deeding to him the Rancho Amigos property, plus adjacent land that I had purchased as a buffer (some 1500 acres). He could therefore be considered a *patron*, with a ranch of his own. Rigo acknowledged this gift, but again showed little emotion or words in expressing his obvious appreciation. Some months later Cyril and I both received an identical letter from Rigo. He had apparently called upon his daughter-in-law, who lives (and was born) in the Rio Grande Valley of Texas, for assistance in preparing it. I say this because it was written in English and expressed quite clearly what would have been most difficult for Rigo to convey, in Spanish or in English. We knew, however, that the sentiments were his alone. It read as follows:

February 14, 1996

Gentlemen:

Thank you very much for directing "Club de Amigos." I would like to extend my gratitude to you for having put up with me for thirty long years uninterruptedly. I appreciate the economic support you were able to provide me and my family.

I remain a little sad, but also realize that all things must come to an end.

Rigo

Of all the wonderful letters I have received in my life, none has meant more than this simple message. Whenever I read it, I remember all the experiences, all the camaraderie, all the obstacles that had to be overcome—and the pure joy we felt through all of it. Most of all, however, I remember Rigo; I will cherish this special bond of friendship forever.

Doves: A Love Affair

My very first game bird was a Mourning Dove, in 1946. If fate is kind to me, my life will end at some South Texas water hole, having a final rendezvous with this same old friend. It would be a fitting way to go: with a smile on my face, saying thanks for the memories.

Without question, this bird and its cousin, the White-winged Dove, have done most to instill in my heart and mind the passion I feel for shooting. While the mystique of shooting has led me to sixteen countries stretching over four continents, engaging along the way a marvelous assortment of game birds, none of these experiences can supplant the bedrock foundation of dove hunting in Texas and Mexico. To the extent that Diana is my alter ego, these two doves are primarily responsible. Why should this love affair be so lasting? Perhaps Darrell Royal put his finger on it when he said, "We should dance with who brung us." These birds "brought me to the party."

It is rare that an old geezer like me, who has hunted birds all his life, does not have a favorite type of shooting—one at which he performs best, or perhaps one that encompasses a setting that fills him with joy. Since all sorts of shooting appeal to me, I am partially the exception in one sense; but if the weight of countless happy memories is the criterion for judgment, then I must place dove as numero uno. Not only have I spent more days afield shooting dove (this fact itself a great plus), but they have also provided rich, challenging variety in a diversity of locations. It would be fatuous to broach the subject of greatest difficulty. We could all make a case for which avian adversary has made us look the most foolish lately. But given the right wind conditions, topography, and other variables of context, these two *palomas* can hold their heads high.

Perhaps we should examine briefly some technical differences and similarities between Mourning Dove (*Zenaida macroura*) and White-winged Dove (*Zenaida asiatica*). The White Wing is definitely larger—by weight about 15 to 20 percent. Not only is it larger, but more closely related (morphologically) to pigeons than to other members of the *Zenaida* genus. Both are compatible with agriculture, Mourning Dove especially so. White Wing suffer from loss of suitable nesting habitat, whereas Mourning Dove are much more flexible in siting their nests. It is encouraging, however, that White Wing seem to be expanding their range into Texas, even as numbers are declining in parts of Mexico where extensive destruction of nesting habitat has occurred. Both normally produce two eggs with each nesting, and both breed seasonally only in the northern portions of their respective ranges. It is not uncommon for Mourning Dove to nest four times annually in our southern states. The nominate race of White-winged Dove (*Zenaida asiatica asiatica*) nests in large, densely populated colonies; the race *mearnsi* (found in our desert southwest and western Mexico) is usually not a colonial nester, nor is the Mourning Dove. Migration is well defined only for the northern population

(South Texas and northeast Mexico) of the nominate race of White-winged Dove, and for those Mourning Dove that breed in our northern states and southern Canada.

As game birds, other differences are quite evident. White Wing often move about in large flights of fifteen to thirty or more birds, particularly when coming into grain fields to feed. Mourning Dove more commonly fly in pairs or in smaller flights, but often singly. The flight characteristics are also distinct. The White Wing's flight is heavy and direct, as compared to the more buoyant flight of Mourning Dove. Both are capable of effective diversionary tactics. When in large flights at fairly close range, White Wing react as a group, diving to present a demanding second shot. Mourning Dove can maneuver quickly and erratically when the shooter comes into view. Both of these doves, which fly at the same approximate normal speed, can be easy targets when flying into the wind or approaching a water hole to drink. But each is brilliantly challenging when flying at above thirty yards, or sliding downwind at perhaps seventy miles per hour.

Some say that one goes dove shooting and quail hunting. I am inclined to dispute this frequent assertion, however, by interpreting hunting in a broad spectrum. A knowledgeable dove aficionado hunts dove in the sense of learning feeding habits, carefully observing flight paths, and placing himself in appropriate positions beneath the invisible "highways" that are used with some semblance of regularity. He also knows that he must move his position with subtle wind vagrancies and time of day. Finally, a dove hunter must learn precisely the effective range at which a bird can be consistently taken—a judgment that involves years of experience, plus a knowledge of shotgun choke, patterns, and size of shot. Based on my experience with sporting-clay shooters and dove hunters of like skill, the experienced dove hunter will usually put twice as many birds in the bag as the shooter who does not possess the hunting talents that have been honed by years in the field.

Since I have been shooting these two doves for over five decades, it would be redundant and tedious to recount even a portion of great shoots I have been privileged to enjoy. Instead, I will only recite four instances, which perhaps will demonstrate the variety of shots that may occur, and why dove shooting can be such a splendid challenge.

White Wing—Wind-Driven and Incoming

Cyril and I often shot shoulder to shoulder at Rancho Amigos in Mexico. We privately called these occasions "mano a mano" competitions: hand to hand engagements. Actually, they were not competitions at all. We sought out the most difficult spot we could locate and then took turns shooting, which gave us the double pleasure of watching each other in action. Our enjoyment came not from numbers, but from the satisfaction of executing a complex shot—the kind that would prompt us to say, "Well done, my friend."

One windy afternoon near a large grain field, Rigo had completed his usual professional job of placing our guests in strategically advantageous locations for maximum opportunities. As was our custom, Cyril and I watched from a vantage point to determine how the White Wing would work in the wind. We noticed that some flocks were flying rapidly downwind to the same area, in an evasive maneuver. We moved to a spot just below a gentle ridge covered with *monte* (thornbrush vegetation) and in line with these downwind comets. A cleared area in front of us separated our shooting position from the ridge. For the next hour we were treated to downwind White Wing that just cleared the ridge as they hurtled directly toward us. We took our usual alternate shots, mano a mano. It was necessary to pick these incomers up just as they cleared the ridge, so that they would fall in the cleared area, or just at our feet. We likened the action to driven Gray Partridge in Britain. It is rare that any game bird will present sustained downwind shooting, since birds ordinarily prefer the greater lift afforded by upwind flight. What a rare opportunity this was! It demanded instant reaction and aggressive movement of the left hand to direct our shots. The winner in this "competition" was the gallant White Wing.

White Wing—Super High Birds

We nearly always had opportunities for high White Wing. It was, in fact, a regular lecture at Rancho Amigos to admonish new shooters that flights seemingly too high were normally within range. I will always remember one group of guests from the Midwest who were all veteran trap shooters but had never shot White Wing. On our first morning's shoot, they simply refused to mount their guns, insisting that the White Wing flights were out of range. Cyril's frustration finally got the best of him. He politely asked if he might test matters out. A guest smugly handed him his gun, whereupon Cyril doubled on the very next flight. The astonished audience of eight guns were not only impressed, but then began to perform quite competently themselves. My private comment to Adams was that he was damned lucky . . . but a not-to-be-ignored instructor. The truth of the matter is that high-flying doves directly overhead look tiny (and out of range), but they may actually be only thirty yards up. High doves create an optical illusion.

On the occasion that I have labeled super-high birds, we took matters to the ultimate extreme. Our group of guests were shooting around a large stock tank. On one side of this body of water the ground fell off noticeably—probably fifteen yards below the dam that created this impoundment. Cyril and I positioned ourselves in this depression some five hundred yards from the other shooters. A major flyway was immediately above the stock tank and continued directly in line with the depression. We were looking at birds a solid forty yards above us as they passed in a steady stream. At first, our mano a mano produced only the odd bird, but in time we found the range. For the next hour or so we rather consistently dropped White Wing from the seemingly endless flights. We estimated the effective leads to be around fifteen feet! Shooting of this sort demands concentration and a steady swing, but it is perfectly doable. It gives one a sense of pride exceeded only by admiration for the doves that make it possible.

Mourning Dove in a Gale

Windy days can be a blessing or a curse, depending upon the bird being pursued. For example, I find high wind quite annoying when hunting quail, for the birds are hard to find, and they scatter badly after flushing. Singles are difficult to work. But a windy day can add a wonderful shooting challenge to most any dove hunt.

Some years ago, my son Stewart and I decided that the two of us would make a February weekend hunt at Rancho Amigos. Although we usually took guests along for our Tamaulipas junkets, we thought it would be nice to have a father-son shoot, with Rigo along to join us. On the first day, we shot quail primarily, finishing up with late afternoon Mourning Dove at a water hole near Rancho Amigos. During the night, a strong front moved through from the northwest—a real "blue norther." By midmorning, the north wind was howling twenty-five miles per hour, gusting to forty. Quail were out of the question, but Rigo had in mind a ranch some ten miles away where he had seen doves feeding in a stubble field. When we reached this destination, dust was blowing badly, but doves were incredibly abundant. I have always felt that Mourning Dove fly more erratically in colder weather, high wind or not. We had both.

We shot for several hours at targets that looked more like windblown, gray ghosts than *palomas*. I can remember no shooting experience more exciting. Most of the birds were sliding crosswind, or falling off downwind, since they could make scant progress upwind. Rigo seldom shows emotion, yet he enjoyed this spectacle with obvious pleasure. The occasional solid hit evoked from him a *"bueno."* We had no bird boys to help us retrieve, and some well-struck doves blew forty to fifty yards before crashing into the ground, but Rigo's sharp eyes assured that no birds were lost. There have been many days when I have relished shooting doves in the wind, but the conditions in this instance made for the best of the best.

Mourning Dove at Dawn

For some reason that I have never understood, most Texas dove hunters do not avail themselves of the opportunity to shoot Mourning Dove at dawn. Perhaps the basis for this oversight is that for years Mourning Dove could be shot only in the afternoon. Thank goodness these regulations were changed.

Morning shoots are ordinarily of less duration than the extended period of feeding and watering in the afternoon, but the quality of shooting can often eclipse the lazier birds of warm late afternoons, especially on a still day. From time to time, the action at dawn can be outstanding, as in the following occasion. Gayle Morton and Cyril had joined Myra and me for a nice coed weekend during the January portion of our split dove season. Our hunting lease was on the West Ranch near Charlotte, Texas, just an hour south of San Antonio. We arose at an early hour in order to be in position at first light. The weather was crisp and clear, except for a few winter clouds in the east. The early hour was cause for some good-natured grumbling, as other hunters ritually inundate me with snide comments about arriving in the dark to shoot doves. I can ignore these barbs by anticipating how enjoyable my dawn cigar will be.

We positioned ourselves safely apart in an extended line near and along a border fence, because Pat West's neighbor had an adjoining field that was completely overgrown with croton (often called goat weed or dove weed). On the preceding afternoon, we had noticed hundreds of doves perched on power lines that roughly paralleled the border fence. We therefore knew this field was a prime feeding location. Mourning Dove in very early light remind me of bats as they come in, usually rather low. They are tough to see and ridiculously difficult to hit, and even to find after they are hit. On this day we had great fun attempting shots and alerting one another to approaching flights. As the sun moved up in the sky, we were witness to a truly spectacular South Texas sunrise, for the clouds took on breathtaking, changing hues.

The flights of doves began to elevate, as they could distinguish our silhouettes. This diversionary action gave us opportunity for some marvelous high passing shots. I could watch with pride as my little bride "worried down" one high bird after another, smartly centering her fair share. After no more than an hour and a half, the action dwindled to a trickle. Within a few minutes, we finished the job, started earlier, of picking and cleaning our birds. By 9:30 A.M. we were in Linda's Cafe just down the road having huevos rancheros and beef tacos for a late breakfast. Can life get better than this?

The above samplings may convey why dove shooting ranks so high in my esteem. Mourning Dove were the starting point of my shooting life and will likely be the last bird that falls to my gun. It is seldom possible, it seems, to return to a point of beginning. Such a rare opportunity came my way in 1996. Most of my earliest dove-shooting experiences took place in the Texas Panhandle on a ranch called Turkey Track, owned by the Whittenberg family. It was leased at that time to Mr. Bill Gunn, as related in the preface. One of the current Whittenberg heirs is Jack Turner, who also happens to be a close friend of my nephew, Tripp Braden. On the fiftieth anniversary of my first dove shoot at Turkey Track, Jack graciously invited my back for a déjà vu extraordinaire. I was joined by my close friend, Jerry Derouen, of Lake Charles, who had been Jack's host shooting snipe in Louisiana.

As we descended from the plains surrounding the ranch into the broken drainage, a tributary of the Canadian River, memories flooded back of my youth and the happy times I had spent on this ranch with Mr. Gunn. The same ancient cottonwood trees lined the watercourses, seemingly as old as the mesas that interrupted the horizon. A new lake or two had been built along the principal watercourse, but stock tanks of smaller sizes were still located on the smaller tributaries. Patches of sunflowers dotted the landscape, reminding me of how I first learned that this plant is a favorite source of seed for Mourning

Dove. We toured this magnificent ranch for several hours before returning to ranch headquarters, where we were graciously accommodated for the weekend.

Late in the afternoon, Jack took us to separate stock tanks, just as dove began to water. The excitement came in remembering how this thrilled a lad of fifteen, who would have spent all afternoon walking along the cottonwoods hoping to get a fleeting shot as doves were flushed ahead. The late afternoon water hole shoot was always icing on the cake. Fifty years of experience had collapsed the time it took me to bag a limit: only some thirty minutes now. It was delicious, however, to stand and watch more and more doves coming to water. Restraint was much easier at sixty-five than at age fifteen, when each bird put in the bag was a source of pride and accomplishment. My thoughts were also filled with dove-shooting memories that connected then and now. It made me want to salute every Mourning Dove and every White-winged Dove that I have ever pursued, for it has truly been a love affair.

The Professional

Who would you name as the most competent person you have ever known? I define competence in a broad sense, as opposed to exceptional proficiency in one area. And we must eliminate Leonardo da Vinci, if we limit ourselves to an individual we have known personally. For some readers, this choice might prove to be a demanding exercise. Not so for me. Without a moment's hesitation or blink, I would name Stewart Campbell.

Unfortunately, there are probably not many of you who know Stewart, unless you are a big-game fisherman—unlikely for readers of a book on bird hunting. His reputation and his many records in this saltwater field of endeavor are well chronicled, but again, I am considering overall competence. I have never known anyone who is even close to being so consistently good at everything he undertakes as Stewart Campbell. If I didn't admire him so much, I would despise him. Color me green with envy. Here are a few of his accomplishments and attributes:

- First in his class in mechanical engineering, University of Texas, 1953.

- Compressor salesman without peer when with Cooper-Bessemer—while still in his twenties.
- Entrepreneur extraordinaire—two highly successful companies brought to fruition and then sold, and not for peanuts.
- A practical mechanic of great talent.
- An exemplary dog trainer who understands the very workings of the canine mind.
- Perhaps the world's premier bill fisherman, holding ten IGFA world records.
- Unfailingly good judgment, including assessment of people.
- The kind of man who leads people so skillfully that they scarcely recognize they are being lead, yet keeps his personal army tightly bound by loyalty—and happy to join him in any enterprise.
- Impeccable personal integrity and commitment to his friends.
- An inquisitive mind that absorbs and holds significant points, dismissing what is unimportant or impractical.
- The coolness of a Clint Eastwood character, which masks a relentless determination to accomplish what happens to be in his sights.
- A good sense of humor.
- The best damned duck hunter I have ever known.

There is much more that could be said about this entirely professional man, but my focus is on the last assertion: duck hunter nonpareil. He started from scratch, which is to say that he received no tutelage from a grizzled waterfowling mentor, or even an ungrizzled one. Like most all else in his life, he made his own observations, formed his own decisions, and perfected his own techniques, with the same fastidious attention to detail that characterizes his modus operandi. Once he decided that duck hunting was a challenge, he chose a unique, difficult environment and then set about to master it in his usual thoughtful manner.

It started out innocently enough. As a youngster in Houston with extremely limited resources, he haunted nearby coastal communities doing odd jobs, which brought him squarely into contact with the powerful hunting and fishing legacy of the Texas Gulf Coast. A favorite locale was Port O'Connor. He was therefore exposed to one of the most productive waterfowl areas in the country. Unfortunately, his opportunities to hunt ducks were as limited as his resources, but he made mental notes for the future. After college, he spent a couple of years in California, before being transferred back to Houston. But now he was the proud owner of a decent shotgun and well on the road to a most successful business career.

Stewart more or less backed into serious duck hunting. He had always had an interest in dogs and an amazing aptitude for training them. With typical thoroughness, he carefully researched how and where to buy a Labrador retriever with a solid pedigree. The end result was a pup that he named Tar. He then turned his attention to training Tar himself, aided only by what he learned from books and what he could glean from local trainers, plus his own indisputable talent. In due course, Stewart and Tar entered retriever field-trial competition, where they enjoyed almost immediate success, starting in the late 1960s and ending rather tragically in the early 1970s. Of the last seven trials in which he was entered, Tar either won or placed second. Unfortunately, when he was only five, his eyesight began to fail, and Stewart was ultimately faced with a heartbreaking euthanasia decision as the malady progressed to blindness.

During this period, Stewart met Lewis Callahan, who also trained dogs and made the field-trial circuit. They soon became fast friends. It was only natural that they should begin hunting ducks together, along with their fine retrievers. They concentrated on the coastal mainland near Port O'Connor, experiencing reasonable success there and meeting several other diehard duck hunters. A mutual friend had introduced them to a rare personality by the name of Jerome "Jebo" Heil and to a high school biology teacher, Houston Riefkohl, to whom they assigned the sobriquet "Reef." Rounding out this assortment of aspiring waterfowlers was Bob McKee, who was another of Callahan's friends from retriever trials. It was an interesting group. They had no other parallel interests or backgrounds, save for the common denominator of duck hunting.

Jebo, who was a framing contractor by trade, was an iron man. He may have been, in those years spanning the 1970s and 1980s, the toughest and most practically direct man I have ever come across. I would definitely want him on my side in a street fight, yet it was his uncommon ability to bull his way through difficult tasks that contributed so much to the group. Callahan was no pansy himself. I always thought of him as the Marlboro Man: a diamond in the rough with intense personal loyalties. He drove a wholesale food distribution truck serving supermarkets during most of the years he hunted with Stewart. I could always count on Callahan. Reef came to the party as a friend of Jebo Heil. I would never have suspected that he taught school or would later become a high school principal, but his great love of duck hunting made him fit in naturally. He seemed to belong to the group. The real anomaly was Bob McKee. Although his successful business career was evidenced by his ultimate position as treasurer and vice president of Transco Oil and Gas, he had none of the practical skills to make much of a contribution to the team. But he loved to duck hunt. Jebo labeled him "the dog," and he was assigned the menial task of food purchasing and preparation, which he just barely managed to accomplish. I found his genial good humor to be a worthy enough addition.

There was little doubt that Stewart was the glue and the undesignated leader of this motley, diverse crew. He was so low key in assuming this role that a casual observer might not be aware that it was his vision and his competence that gave the operation direction. Shortly after the group coalesced, they decided that Matagorda Island would be prime duck-hunting territory, but this extensive barrier island had formidable natural features and logistical problems of access that made it generally impractical to hunt on a regular basis. It was a challenge made for the inventive mind of Stewart Campbell.

Matagorda Island became property of the Federal government during World War II, during which time an air base of second-tier importance was constructed on the high-ground, western end of the island. After the war, ownership and management was disputed between the State and the Feds for many years. During this period of controversy, it was generally (but not conclusively) agreed that the State would control the eastern sector—mostly tidal salt marsh— while the U.S. Fish and Wildlife would retain ownership and management of the higher ground on the west end. The entire length of Matagorda Island is about thirty miles. The eastern marshy portion, most important for wintering waterfowl, is about ten miles in length, and not much more than a mile in width. Finally, during the administration of Governor Clements, it was agreed that Texas Parks and Wildlife would assume responsibility for management of the entire island, with the Federal government retaining its ownership.

Stewart and his crew were, of course, focused on the salt marsh, which was home to thousands of ducks overwintering on the Texas coast. It was inhospitable for several reasons. The normal depth is only about six inches, perfect for the reach of dabbling ducks but hardly navigable for boats of any consequence. Tidal fluctuation is only a matter of inches, but sustained strong winds can affect depths by a foot or more, which makes any one location for a blind an impossible puzzle. In addition, the salt marsh itself is a labyrinth of waterways through grassy isles of slightly higher terrain, punctuated by sections of open water. Since recognizable landmarks are almost totally lacking, the average person finds it hopelessly difficult to navigate this maze. It is a network so complex that only a few dedicated individuals have mastered its intricacies. And imagine how impossible it becomes in dense fog, when even the comfort of distant landmarks are nonexistent. For the most part the bottom consists of a muddy, organic ooze into which one can sink to his midcalf with every step. When disturbed, this surface layer gives off a strong hydrogen sulfide odor, confirming its organic nature.

But if inhospitable to man, the salt marsh is a paradise for wildlife. Aside from duck, it is frequented by a dazzling assortment of shorebirds (migrating and resident), heron and egret, geese, raptor, many varieties of salt-marsh-oriented passerine, and even (from time to time) that symbol of rarity and protection: the magnificent Whooping Crane. Fishermen treasure the marsh as perfect habitat for runs of redfish. Interestingly, it is also home to a few hardy mammals, such as raccoons, muskrats, and numerous rodents, plus coyotes, deer, and rabbits on areas of higher ground. Oh yes, it is renowned for its exceptional density of rattlesnakes, which can pop up most anywhere, but especially in any area not usually submerged.

The first problems to be solved by the Campbell clan were: how to access the island, penetrate the salt marsh, and move about within the shallow maze (often only mudflats). The first part was relatively easy. After operating for a time out of a motel in Port Lavaca and reaching Matagorda Island by means of a venerable Boston whaler, they determined that lodging closer to the island was needed. This decision meant building a large, barge-mounted

houseboat and docking it at a fishing camp called Bob and Leonard's, which is located on the Intracoastal Waterway some fifteen miles west of Port O'Connor. This base camp suited their purposes well for many years. It was only a two-mile whaler run to the point on Matagorda where they could enter the salt marsh. Internal mobility was another issue. In the late 1960s airboats were little more than a novelty; the light-weight scooters used in areas like the Everglades were totally inadequate for their purposes and for conditions that existed on Matagorda.

Fortunately, Stewart heard of a boat builder by the name of Tolbert Crowder in Port Arthur, Texas, who was experimenting with a large, sturdy airboat, with a stepped-hull design that showed great promise for the type of salt marsh along the Texas coast. It was powered by a rather standard Lycoming aircraft engine, utilizing a single-bladed, wooden, aircraft propeller. Variations of this original design served the group well for the next twenty-five years. Later versions took advantage of emerging fiberglass technology and modifications based on hard-won experience, but this basic craft was ideal. Although heavy and somewhat awkward to remove if jammed into a muddy bank, it could fly across the shallow water at fifty miles per hour and seemed to pick up speed on slick mudflats.[1] Moreover, it could hold four hunters with gear and decoys quite well, almost comfortably except for the noise. To protect himself against declining availability of the Lycoming engine, which inevitably had to be replaced as the brutal saltwater environment (along with extended usage) took its toll, Stewart wisely located an Army Surplus source and bought six or seven at $100 each, some of which still remain in warehouse storage.

[1] *Through a friend on his staff, I came to know Admiral Roy Johnson, who was then the Five-Star Commander of the Pacific Fleet—and also an avid bird hunter. On one of the several occasions that he was my guest in Texas, I asked Stewart if we could include him on a Matagorda Island duck hunt, which worked out perfectly as I knew it would. But Admiral Johnson's greatest fascination was with the airboat. Stewart made a notable exception and let him fly it. Here was a man who had piloted every aircraft available to the Navy and whose flagship was a supercarrier, yet he delighted in maneuvering the airboat over the shallows and mudflats, like a kid with a new toy.*

After mastering how to pilot the airboat (which sometimes had a mind of its own), conquering all of the myriad mechanical field repair requirements, and learning how to negotiate the complex labyrinth of the Matagorda Island saltwater marsh, Stewart and his cohorts were faced with the next obstacle: deciding on the type and location of duck blinds. It was an evolutionary process, complete with natural selection. Stewart was appalled by what others had attempted in past isolated efforts to hunt the Matagorda marsh. These old blinds consisted of wooden frames covered usually with chicken wire so that broom grass or cattails could be inserted around the periphery to hide the shooters. He termed these "hot dog stands," for they were so obviously out of place in the low saltwater marsh. They seemed to call attention to themselves, as if to say, "Here we are; avoid us." Stewart was convinced that any effective blind would have to be buried, but this concept introduced a whole new set of problems.

They first tried 55-gallon metal drums, cut in back so that a seat could be notched out, and fitted on the bottom with wooden extensions to prevent them from popping up. It was a great idea but unsuccessful over any extended period: The saltwater ate up the metal, and the blinds invariably floated under storm tide conditions. The next approach was more satisfactory. These blinds were precast concrete, elliptical in cross section, and included a cast-in-place seat. The advantage was that they were heavy enough not to float, since each barrel weighed 800 pounds; the disadvantage was the agony of handling these monsters, transporting them across the bay, and burying them in the mud. Besides, Stewart (ever the perfectionist) did not like their appearance from above: too large an opening from a duck's overhead perspective in flight.

Finally they hit upon a workable alternative design, made of fiberglass, which proved to be the solution to all these problems. The configuration was pure genius. Each individual blind was shaped like the early space capsules (or like the Erlenmeyer flasks used in chemistry labs): conical but truncated, with

a cylindrical entrance shaft. This shape, when buried, insured that the blind would not float out, because of the heavy mud bearing down on the conical flare. The opening to the cylindrical top was small and easy to disguise, and the flare of the cone gave ample leg room. An inverted bucket (needed anyway for bailing) made a perfect seat. A local boat builder, Willis Hudson, could mold the fiberglass over a sheet-metal frame with relative ease, leaving out the bottom for removal of the form, and adding it as a second step. Fiberglass, of course, was not subject to saltwater corrosion.

How and where to place blinds was yet another challenge. Over the years, Stewart had carefully observed patterns of feeding ducks: the exact depth of water preferred; how water depth changed with different wind and tide conditions and caused duck concentrations to shift; and how physical configuration of the marsh and sections of open water affected the placement of decoys, impacting attractiveness to passing flights of ducks. Naturally, no one location would fit diverse wind and tide conditions, nor allow for the preferences of ducks on any given day. Stewart is also a pilot and owned at this time a small Piper Supercub. He spent endless hours flying slowly over the salt marsh studying where large rafts of ducks were likely to form under varying circumstances. Not much was left to chance in siting the blinds.

Putting blinds in place was a gruesome chore. It was usually undertaken in summer months, making it even more hellish. Digging in this horrible mud and ooze was exhausting, which prompted numerous ideas about an easier approach. Stewart even hit upon the inspiration of using dynamite, which was tried, but this noble plan failed because a charge placed deep enough blew out a huge cavity. The resulting crater then required an agonizing amount of back-fill, not to mention destruction of the surrounding marsh grass. They ultimately settled on an effective, but labor-intensive, method. First, it was necessary to build a cofferdam around the location selected for the blind. As man-powered excavation took place, water within the cofferdam had to be bailed out. When the cofferdams were deep enough, the fiberglass capsules were then set in place and backfilled with mud that had been excavated. Two individual capsules were ordinarily set side by side, or occasionally in a cluster of three. About forty-two individual barrels were buried at about twenty locations. The top level of the entrance cylinder was set a scant three to four inches above normal high tide. This low freeboard meant that water often filled the capsule, but bailing was not an onerous or time-consuming chore.

Stewart was particularly fussy about disguising the blinds. From another location, he would pull clumps of the ubiquitous *Spartina patens* (commonly called salt marsh cordgrass), and then replant it around the blinds. By the time duck season opened, each blind was buried in a surrounding of completely natural cordgrass. They were virtually invisible, except from directly above, and then not conspicuous. Various types of camouflage jackets and caps were compared so that the ultimate choice blended perfectly, insuring that ducks would sense nothing as they decoyed.

Decoy types and numbers were also carefully evaluated. In the early days they used conventional decoys but then came to realize that ducks on Matagorda Island were attracted to large rafts, whether of other ducks or rafts of coots. It was quite expensive to put out 200 to 300 decoys at two or three locations, so they tried using gallon cans painted to simulate Northern Pintail, at least roughly. In practice, this ruse worked rather well, but maintenance was a royal pain. It was finally decided to "hang the cost" and use quality decoys. Handling such a large number of decoys had its own logistical problems. By this time the Campbell clan had two airboats, but it was still difficult to accommodate some 400 to 500 decoys. A single innovation greatly reduced the hassle. They discovered that 18-inch lengths of thick (about $3/16$ of an inch) nylon cording with an O-ring lead weight on the end worked perfectly to hold the decoys in place, and could be transported much easier on the bow and interior storage of the airboats. These lines (dyed green, later dulled with mud) were never wrapped around the decoys until stored after the season. They were simply removed from the water and placed carefully on (or in) the airboats. There was little tendency to tangle.

Picture, then, the strategy and scene on any given occasion. Stewart would usually fly the island on the day before hunting was to begin, noting where ducks were feeding and which sets of blinds should be most productive. It was not necessary to begin shooting at dawn, because Matagorda's ducks generally returned to mainland, freshwater sites to drink late in the afternoon, where they remained until the following morning. Large flights returned to the saltwater marsh to feed about eight in the morning. Sometimes the decoys were left in place from the preceding day, but Stewart always seemed to have some sense about why they should be moved to a different location because of wind or tide. They were set in place in a massive U, with one leg shorter than the other and this leg leading into the wind. Such a configuration gave a large number of decoying ducks ample room to land.

Ordinarily two guns, dropped off by the airboat at any given blind location, would bag a limit in short order, and hunters could be rotated until everyone had an opportunity to shoot. It was not the practice to pick up ducks that fell, for three reasons: It was exhausting to do so; downed birds floated only a short distance across open water until they hung up on marsh grass, where they could easily be retrieved by airboat; and unnecessary traffic in and out of the blinds damaged the natural cover. Decoys were set out and picked up using the airboat to minimize walking in the soft mud. Unlike duck hunting in a freshwater setting, it was not important to call. Pintail and widgeon are sometimes responsive to a whistle, but experience on Matagorda suggested that large spreads of decoys, well placed, made calling a redundancy.

On rare occasions ducks would ignore a beautiful invitation to a well-selected location. If two or three flights passed us by, our leader was quick to take the hint and we would gather up all the decoys and move. He had learned from hard experience that waterfowl have minds of their own, and at times base choice on some factor known only to them. We would move to where ducks were working. Most of the guests who shot with Stewart were unfamiliar with this type of operation and could contribute little. Jebo, Callahan, and Stewart made it all look easy. An experienced duck hunter, however, knew better, and could well appreciate the amount of preparation, knowledge, and advance effort that was involved.

The ducks themselves were unbelievable, both in quantity and variety. In the late 1960s, '70s, and '80s, probably 40 percent were Northern Pintail, 30 percent or so American Widgeon, 15 to 20 percent Redheads, and the remaining 10 to 15 percent a variety of species, but mainly Green-winged Teal, Gadwall, Mottled Duck, and Northern Shoveler. This is not to say that Mallard, Canvasback, Blue-winged Teal, Cinnamon Teal, Ruddy Duck, Lesser Scaup, Bufflehead, and Common Goldeneye were unlikely to be seen on any given day. Black Duck and Eurasian Widgeon were accidental rarities, but not out of the question. Part of the pleasure of shooting with this knowledgeable crew was the emphasis they put on waterfowl identification, and the unwritten rules they placed on which ducks could be shot.

Redheads were definitely taboo, not so much for the restrictions imposed by the State and Feds, but because they were considered too dumb. You could almost count on a flight of Redheads "taking off your cap" as you were setting out decoys. You could stand up in the blind and wave your arms, and they would still decoy. Principal focus was on drake pintail and drake widgeon. It was acceptable to accidentally shoot a hen widgeon, but a hen pintail was a definite no-no. Teal and Gadwall were permissible sport shooting, but generally frowned upon. The odd Mottled Duck was also acceptable. A spoonie (Northern Shoveler) was considered a good joke, subjecting the shooter to ridicule but not admonishment.

For several years, a "kitty" jar was prominently displayed in the houseboat. We were fined $5 for a hen pintail, $2 for a hen widgeon, and $10 for a Redhead. This feature was more a gentle embarrassment than a serious assessment. It prompted an amusing response from a good friend, Dick Skinner, who is a delightful gentleman and a highly respected businessman. These qualities notwithstanding, Dick couldn't tell a Mallard from a Bufflehead, much less identify them in flight. He expressed his frustration with the rules by saying, "Could I just put $100 in the kitty and shoot anything that comes by?"

Stewart and his associates were kind enough to invite Cyril and me to shoot at Matagorda dozens of times. We loved the pageantry and the professionalism as much as the actual shooting. The sulfide smell of the salt marsh, originally offensive, came to be an almost symbolic, sensual pleasure, since it was invariably associated with good times, good friends, and good experiences. It was often our practice, after collecting a limit in less than a hour, to put aside our guns and observe the interaction of wildlife in the salt marsh. Particularly fascinating was to watch huge pintail and widgeon flights come into the decoys and land. On one memorable occasion, Stewart and I sat side by side in the blind as perhaps a thousand ducks settled in front of us. And what, in all of waterfowling, can be more spectacular than Northern Pintail dropping from the heights with their wings cupped in a fashion that distinguishes them from all other ducks? Perhaps incidents such as this, coupled with meeting the challenges of shooting there, made it all worthwhile for the Professional and his associates.

Unfortunately, it all came to an end in the 1990s. Jebo moved to the East Coast, where apartment-framing opportunities could not be overlooked. Callahan was stricken with lung cancer, and we all lost a valued friend. Airboats of more advanced design became available to the general public, and heavy traffic virtually ruined what had been a waterfowl paradise on Matagorda Island. Stewart became more and more involved in breaking billfish records, and lost, when Callahan died, some of his zeal for duck hunting. A new era may be dawning, however. His grandchildren are reaching shooting age, and he has recently purchased significant acreage just west of Port O'Connor, where he has a beautiful second home. Several freshwater ponds are located on this new property, and I feel sure he will soon turn his attention to making it a duck hunting heaven for his progeny—and I hope for me also.

I should share one last happening in particular that illustrates how powerful the bond of friendship can become between sportsmen who hunt together over many years. One November day, Callahan and the Dog (Bob McKee) were hunting together when a change in weather dropped the temperature suddenly, and a dense fog shrouded Matagorda Island late in the day. They became hopelessly lost, not having Stewart's uncanny navigational skills. Wisely, they cut the airboat's engine to conserve fuel and waited for a change in conditions. But it was now bitterly cold and they were not suitably dressed. Around midnight, someone at Bob and Leonard's noticed that Callahan and McKee had not returned from Matagorda. About one o'clock in the morning, they called Stewart in Houston to report that his buddies were missing. Imagine being awakened at such an hour with this news.

Houston is about three and a half hours from Bob and Leonard's, and the weather was abominable. Stewart hesitated not a minute, stopping only long enough to call Jebo, saying he would pick him up on the way. They reached the houseboat around four o'clock and struck off across the bay for the island, still in dense fog. It is beyond my comprehension to think that they could find the only feasible entry into the salt marsh, much less locate their friends in the interior labyrinth, yet they had no thoughts of doing otherwise—needle in the haystack be damned.

From time to time they would cut the engine of their air-boat to listen for Callahan and the Dog. About an hour before dawn, Callahan started his airboat for another futile try at finding their way out. Miraculously, Stewart and Jebo heard them far in the distance, and were able to close the range by stopping at intervals to listen. Finally they could see the fire from the exhaust and could pull alongside. "How are the ducks working?" said Jebo as he threw them warm jackets. Just as remarkable as the rescue was Stewart's ability then to exit the foggy marsh at the precise location of the whalers, with apparent ease.

On those occasions when I hear severe criticism of hunters, who are so often characterized as selfish, redneck louts who murder innocent creatures, I think of examples of this sort, which illustrate a powerful sense of personal loyalty. It is also heartening to see individuals of such diverse backgrounds build an edifice of friendship based on a mutual love of hunting. We who have been there know that the purpose of hunting is not killing, but, instead, participating in the natural scene. I am in debt to the Professional for helping me realize this.

Pigeon Preferences: A Triumvirate

In consonance with many before me, I find the family *Columbidae* (pigeons and doves) to be fascinating birds, whether sought after for bird watching or pursued for shooting. One of the most impressive events of my birding career was the lucky sighting of Southern Crowned Pigeon (*Goura sheepmakeri*) in the lowland southern forests of New Guinea. This pigeon is not only rare, but enormous (near turkey size), a beautiful grayish blue specimen with an incredible crest of lacy feathers and a shocking red iris. The many brilliantly colored fruit dove of Asia and Australasia are also breathtaking to behold. But as I am considering pigeons that are also splendid game birds, I choose three members of the genus *Columba* that have provided the most unforgettable shooting experiences. These are the Speckled Pigeon (*Columba guinea*), disjunctly distributed in central and in southern Africa; Picazuro Pigeon (*Columba picazuro*) of southern South America; and Common Wood Pigeon (*Columba palumbus*), which are widely distributed in the entire western Palearctic region.

Of this triumvirate, I must confess that Wood Pigeon most captures my fancy, based on numerous encounters in England, Scotland, and Ireland. However, two profoundly memorable days of shooting were with Speckled Pigeon in South Africa, closely followed in ranking by another day-to-remember with Picazuro Pigeon in the pampas of Argentina. After spending a lifetime shooting Mourning Dove and White-winged Dove in North America, these much larger cousins are impressive, particularly when the setting further heightens the experience.

Cyril Adams and I made our first bird-hunting trip to Africa in 1973, at the invitation of professional hunter Tony Challis, who, along with the South African government, wanted to test the reaction of American sportsmen to a variety of game birds available in the Orange Free State and in the Transvaal. We were, of course, happy to be guinea pigs. It proved to be a marvelous initial trip (the first of several), which gave us an opportunity to taste the delights of shooting African waterfowl, francolin, and guineafowl, in addition to pigeons and doves. Various government representatives accompanied us at times, including an ornithologist at one point. His observations about South African birds significantly added to my pleasure on the trip.

Our first exposure to Speckled Pigeon, known locally as Rock Pigeon, was in commercial sunflower fields near Johannesburg. The race found in South Africa is, incidentally, *Columba guinea phaeonotus*, which is superficially different from the central African *Columba guinea guinea*. The proper common name derives from white spots on the wing secondaries and short white streaks on the neck, giving it a speckled appearance. We were cordially welcomed by the farmers there, since these abundant pigeons were considered more than just casual pests. Upon later examining distended crops (gullets) of these large pigeons, we could understand why their depredations are not well received. The number of large sunflower seeds in each crop was impressive. Our shooting here was interesting and varied, but no more unusual than the familiar Red-billed Pigeons (*Columba flavirostris*) we were accustomed to shooting in the sorghum fields of northeastern Mexico. Our next confrontation was quite another matter.

Tony took us about 150 miles south of Johannesburg to a town by the name of Bethlehem, not to be confused with the biblical village of the same name. Our "Little Town of Bethlehem" hardly brings back happy memories for Cyril, for he was stricken with a raging fever. It was a mysterious malady that haunted him for many years, before and after this African trip. Based on history with previous attacks, we had some confidence that it would run its course quickly, but he was in no condition to leave his room. Tony posted a native chap by his bed with a pitcher of ice water and Cokes and with instructions to provide fluid on a continuing basis, never leaving his side. I gathered that Tony must also have given the aide strong incentive to be faithful, if he desired to continue living himself. We then ventured forth early the following day for what Tony promised to be a quite different look at Rock Pigeon. I felt some remorse at leaving Cyril, but he reassured me with something along the line, "If I die, I die."

We met a local farmer, who was reputed to be an outstanding trap shot, and who was particularly fond of shooting Rock Pigeons. His favorite locations happened to be in the steep escarpments that lead up to the Drakensberg Mountain Range. Although warned by Tony that it would be rough highland country, I was dumbfounded at the setting when we finally arrived. The scene resembled a scaled-down Grand Canyon, with nearly vertical walls, and extending apparently for miles. A small army of native shepherd lads met us at a predetermined rendezvous point, and we set off up the canyon with guns and more shells than I thought could possibly be necessary.

What followed was extraordinary. They dropped me off first with instructions to climb about two-thirds of the way up the canyon wall—and the word climb is no exaggeration, for it was virtually hand over hand. From this point I was to shoot pigeons as they returned from feeding in the valley below, which caused me to wonder, since not a pigeon had we seen. Two other thoughts crossed my mind as I lifted myself up the rock face: Where in the world would I find a place to stand? And how could the birds (if any) be retrieved?

Answers were soon revealed. I finally found a small platform of level ground, with my back to the wall and a drop of several hundred feet in front of me. Shortly after checking out my shooting stand, I noticed two things: Pigeons were beginning to fly up the narrow canyon—good news; and the relative calm of early morning was giving way to an increasingly stiff breeze—bad news. Concerns of bird retrieval were fast being replaced with concern for maintaining my balance on my precarious perch in a wind of 20 to 25 miles per hour. But one does things at forty-two that one does not risk at sixty-seven, so I decided to blast away. It was phenomenal shooting. One pigeon would be straight above me some twenty-five yards, dodging in the wind. The next would be fifty feet or more below me, which presented an entirely different line of flight. Not surprisingly, results from the initial box of shells were not at all commendable, drawing disapproving looks from my entourage of four or five lads. My resolve began to firm as a matter of pride. An experienced Texas dove hunter should be able to kill these big pigeons, despite being terrified by the available footing.

Soon I managed to get the hang of the bizarre variety of wind-driven shots, and birds began to drop—and did they drop, several hundred feet at times! Now my retrieval concerns were answered. The shepherd kids scurried up, down, and across the rocky canyon walls like mountain goats, not missing a bird and seemingly enjoying what looked like agonizing work to me. Our bird boys in Mexico are capable of fine results in their own briar patch of *Tamaulipas monte*, but the topographic considerations here made the degree of difficulty truly astonishing.

In addition to this rugged setting and wonderful flights of birds, each shot produced an echo that reverberated up and down the canyon, answered from time to time by the other guns in the distance. We continued shooting for at least three hours, until the flights tapered off. I was extremely gratified to learn that my bag compared favorably to my hosts, and that the honor of the great state of Texas had not been compromised. The entire experience was one for the memory book, unique to say the least.

It was painful for me to think that Cyril had missed this opportunity. We returned to Bethlehem to see if he had survived the day. We found him much improved, complaining primarily that his "nurse" had nearly drowned him in water and Cokes. His bladder was suffering more than his febrile brow. The faithful attendant seemed much relieved that his own life was to be spared. I dared not report what a splendid day it had been—out of kindness, and out of fear Adams would strangle me.

My next "pigeon preference" requires moving one continent to the west and ten years later in time, to the Pampas of Argentina. But first, a bit of background is in order. Through business connections, I had come to know quite well the CEO of Hughes Tool Company, Mr. Jim Lesch. Jim was not only a highly respected oil industry executive, but was—and is—an excellent shot and a boon hunting companion. If you visualize him to be a polished corporate executive (of the Harvard Business School mold) you would err, for this image does not fit

his personality and demeanor. Here instead is an engineer who rose through the ranks in the oil patch, and
then ascended the corporate ladder to the very top of a
major manufacturing company. His success was accomplished by sole virtue of ability and unfailing good
judgment. Tough, fair, and outspoken come to mind
when describing him.

Hughes Tool (now Baker-Hughes) primarily manufactured oil drilling bits and had facilities located
throughout our country and the world, including Argentina. The corporate offices in Buenos Aires also served
all of South America, and operated autonomously, with
their own board of directors—or at least this was the
case in the 1980s. When Cyril and I expressed an interest in shooting in Argentina, Jim assured us it could be
arranged. We did not realize how well! What we did
not know at the time was that a close friendship existed
between Jim and one of the members of his board,
Federico Paralta-Ramos. We were privileged to meet
this remarkable Argentine a few weeks later on one of
his rather frequent visits to Houston. If Jim Lesch could
be considered at times a bit rough around the edges,
Federico was the very apotheosis of a gentleman, a class
act in every sense. Although an architect by training, he
was truly a renaissance man: fluent in five languages,
formerly a renowned international polo player, an informed student of opera, a respected businessman, a
sportsman (hunter and angler), and a successful rancher.
He was as distinguished in appearance as he was impressive and charming in his dealings with people at
all levels of society. We later had Federico as our guest
at Rancho Amigos in Mexico on many occasions. Notable, and significant to me, was his kindness to Rigo,
other members of our permanent "staff," and even to
the local paisanos.

After meeting him in Houston, we were invited to shoot on his two *estancias* (ranches) in the pampas of the Buenos Aires province of Argentina. As it turned out, this invitation extended as well to the *estancias* of friends in the same region. Myra and I were in the process of a lengthy courtship, which preceded our eventual marriage, and Federico gallantly insisted that she join us, after meeting her in Houston. Including her would result in amusing consequences. When we arrived in Buenos Aires, we were elegantly received by Federico, who introduced us most properly to this sophisticated metropolis. His architectural creations were evident at most every turn.

His primary *estancia* was located about four hours by car from the city, and the ranch house itself was what one would expect of such a man, and far too elegant for the likes of three. Further descriptions of the surrounding wetlands habitat will be reserved for the chapter titled "Ducks and Tinamous in Argentina," but I should mention that we would hardly have expected pigeons in the endless sea of grass that comprises most of the pampas scene. We discovered, however, that shooting *Columbidae* was no different here than elsewhere: a matter of locations that concentrated the birds.

On the afternoon of our arrival, we discovered that the giant evergreens and eucalyptus surrounding the ranch headquarters were roosting habitat for the large and darkly handsome Picazuro Pigeon. They came here by the hundreds. Federico seemed quite surprised to learn that Myra intended to shoot with us. Argentine men are notoriously macho, and in the 1980s had yet to accept women's liberation. Although characteristically gracious, he placed her at a stand on the periphery of the action, out of harm's way. We found the shooting to be most enjoyable, as the pigeons came in high over the treetops, presenting viable, but not unrealistic, targets. After an hour or so, the birds had settled in and we were picked up by the ranch foreman. Last of the shooters in line was Myra. The look on Federico's face when we arrived at her stand was priceless: She is a tiny lady and the pile of birds came almost to her knees. He was simultaneously speechless and caught off guard (for once). Myra smiled brightly and complimented him on a nice presentation. Adams and I were smugly proud of our protégé.

The next couple of days found us seriously engaged in duck hunting, but we then had an invitation to shoot pigeons on the fabulous Estancia Acelain of Agustín Larrata, Federico's friend and a neighboring landowner. On this occasion the setting was entirely different. We were unprepared for the elegance that was to confront us on this *estancia*. It was more of a principality than a ranch, and the headquarters had a striking resemblance to the San Simeon mansion of William Randolph Hearst along the California coast. We were in awe of this world apart from anything the three of us had ever seen. Aside from the marbled palace, state dining rooms, and formal gardens, we were amazed at the complete village of supporting personnel and trades that had for generations been resident here: a self-contained community.

After an impressive luncheon, we were asked if a little sport with pigeons would be of interest to us. Naturally we accepted, but really expected more Picazuro Pigeon coming to roost in the forest of trees that surrounded the headquarters. We were driven instead to a nearby lake. A lengthy embankment, which served as the dam for the impoundment, was lined on its crest with tall trees resembling willows. We were placed below the embankment in a depressed area, at least thirty feet below the crest and sixty feet or more below the tree tops. We expected a few scattered pigeons coming across the lake and over the trees for a sporty diversion. What followed instead was an unremitting stream of pigeons for more than two hours, all passing some ten yards above the trees. It was a dream come true for those who love high, strong-flying birds.

Federico's only "failing" as a superior host and guide was his insistence on supplying us with heavy loads, in spite of our request for 7½ trap loads. My rather light Boss hammer gun took a frightful beating over the constant two hours or so of shooting. It didn't fail me at the time, but both top and bottom ribs had to be resoldered (or retinned, to use the British term) upon our return home, and the hinge pin had worn loose and had to be retightened. Poor Myra suffered far worse than her gun, for her cheek was bruised by the shooting angle (almost straight up). She looked like an abused woman the next day. None of these minor adversities kept us from pounding away, however, for we all realized that such a phenomenon represented a chance of a lifetime.

When the smoke cleared, the smooth grassy area below the embankment looked a bit like a pigeon graveyard, causing us to feel some regret at our own avarice. When our hosts returned, we were relieved to see that they, at least, were highly pleased. Only then did we learn that they customarily feed these "pests" to the pigs. This knowledge only aggravated our sense of guilt. Perhaps we can be excused for our gluttony by the remarkable presentation of birds, unlikely to be repeated in quite this same manner.

The two experiences just described—with Speckled Pigeon in South Africa and Picazuro Pigeon in Argentina—concern two unusual presentations on single occasions in unforgettable settings. Common Wood Pigeon of the western Palearctic, on the other hand, have provided shooting thrills on many a day in the British Isles. This pigeon has, moreover, characteristics that set it apart from other members of this family. First of all, we Americans have an initial difficulty visualizing the proportions of this brute. Perhaps it can best be brought into focus by comparison: something about the size of a plump Blue-winged Teal, or roughly twice the size (in weight, at least) of domestic pigeon (Rock Pigeon). Woodies are easily recognizable by their prominent white collar and white bar at the bend of the wing. When seen, as they often are, in urban areas and parks, they would suggest a rather straight-forward target, like a flying hippo. Not so this illusion when shooting is attempted in feeding or roosting situations.

The fact that all agricultural interests consider this species to be vermin and that it is unprotected at any season has resulted in relentless persecution through-out Britain for over 150 years. Yet the total population, which varies somewhat due to seasonal migrations, re-mains stable in the neighborhood of ten million birds[1]. Some contend that natural selection has made these huge pigeons such canny game birds, able to survive heavy shooting pressures. Whatever the reason, Woodies are certainly one of the wariest of birds. They are both a challenge to bring into range and a challenge to shoot, for they are extremely strong fliers.

Cyril and I had our first exposure to Wood Pigeons on an unusual adventure in 1978. A shooting trip to the UK had long been a priority, but we had neither resources for, nor knowledge of, driven birds at this juncture. Somehow Adams had gotten the name of an estate near Aberdeen called the House of Dunn, which advertised "rough shooting" as avail-able when no driven shoots were scheduled (which turned out to be virtually the entire season). Apparently there had been an untimely death in the family, with the result that the estate, and its driven shooting potential, had suffered badly. As a matter of fact, the only redeeming virtue of the House of Dunn, in 1978, was its proximity to the Glenmorangie distill-ery. But the disheveled condition of the facilities matched well with the gear and appearance of the two itinerant Texans who showed up to sample what might be there in the way

[1] *This population stability is one of the reasons many of us believe that restrictive Mourning Dove limits and seasons in the United States are unrealistic.*

of sport. Looking back at our naiveté, I am appalled at how ill-prepared we were for Scotland in November. We had no rubber boots, no Barbour jackets (or any other reliable rain gear), and nothing warm enough for the predictably unpredictable weather of northern Britain. Two pair of blue jeans, three warm shirts, a light-weight camouflage jacket, and hiking boots composed our essential kit for this expedition. We got soaked on the first afternoon and never really dried out over the next four or five days. We were never warm.

Soon after arrival, we were introduced to a wonderful old Scottish gamekeeper, whose weathered look bespoke decades of experience. He provided us a perfect introduction to shooting in Britain, with sound advice that we would put to future good use. Around midafternoon of our first day, in a steady drizzle of icy rain, he put us into position for our first go at Woodies. We were placed behind a shoulder-high hedgerow that lined a recently cut grain field and were told to conceal ourselves well—advice that we only partially heeded, at first. When the birds began to pass by our stations, we blazed away, fully confident that we would destroy these giant bombers. Nothing fell! It was a downright embarrassment. We were at a complete loss to understand our performance (which precisely matched our miserable condition) until I finally "ragged down" a pigeon. Then it was abundantly apparent what had been amiss: The downed bird was a good fifty to sixty yards from the hedgerow. Because of their enormous size, we had totally misjudged distance, so all of our shots had been out of range. Lesson one about Wood Pigeons was imprinted. Lesson two soon followed: Conceal yourself perfectly and do not move a muscle (or gun) until prepared to shoot. We finished the day with perhaps a dozen birds each—not bad for first-time gringos.

The following day, after walking up Gray Partridge, pheasant, and hare, we were hurried off in late afternoon to a large stand of enormous evergreens that were about fifty feet in height and so densely spaced as to be impenetrable. Through the middle of this small forest was a clear-cut strip, about the width of a narrow roadway. Our gamekeeper explained that Woodies in large numbers came here to roost if not disturbed, and this roost had not been shot for several weeks. He was dead right. Since our stands were along the cleared strip, we had visibility only straight above, which severely limited the amount of time we had to get off a shot at passing pigeons. On the plus side, the birds could not see us until it was too late for more than their usual diversionary tactics. Incidentally, these large pigeons can move laterally instantly, with a flick of their enormous wings. The shooting was truly splendid and our bag respectably greater than the previous day—perhaps thirty to forty birds each. All were smartly retrieved in dense woods by two lovely retrievers in a style that we were to learn is the norm in Britain.

Our experiences with Wood Pigeons at the House of Dunn proved to be typical in many ways to frequent subsequent experiences over the years, except that things were usually much more highly organized on other estates. For example, we learned that gamekeepers carefully scout in advance and build proper individual blinds (called hides in Britain) next to cover in fields that are being used for feeding. Decoys are also a vital part of the equation and add to the drama. We were ordinarily given fifteen or so decoys to be placed in much the same manner as duck decoys, with cognizance of wind. Once a few Woodies are dropped, they are carefully placed among the decoys by propping up their heads with small sticks. The larger the spread, the more effective it becomes, so that, if all goes well, soon flights of fifteen to twenty-five birds decoy perfectly, making it great sport.

It is often possible to shoot roosting sites as well, always a challenge because Wood Pigeons will not chose a roost where it is easy to position yourself. On one occasion we shot from a large platform high in the trees, carefully concealed and putting us almost at eye level with the pigeons. Gamekeepers ordinarily like to arrange these shoots for a modest charge (compared to driven shooting) because they can sell a brace of pigeons for about fifty to seventy pence. Most of the Woodies are marketed to the Continent, where they are apparently considered a more desirable table bird than in Britain.

For me, Wood Pigeons are truly regal game birds—my pigeon preference. They are marvelously strong fliers, wary, and difficult to bring down unless struck well. Moreover, I cannot help but admire how they have successfully matched the will of their adversaries over the years.

Ducks and Tinamous in Argentina

My Argentine friend, Federico Paralta-Ramos of the previous chapter, was always referred to by us as Don Federico, out of respect. Sadly this quintessence of a gentleman-sportsman succumbed to cancer a few years ago, but his stature and innate courtesy were of such depth as to leave a lasting impression, not to be dulled by passage of time.

If his persona manifested the slightest negativity, it was a certain inflexibility in his viewpoints. Or, as we would say in the uncouth world of South Texas, he was hardheaded as hell on some subjects, including hunting and fishing. For example, he was adamant about using cartridges that had brass about midway up the casing of the shell. No amount of reasoning or supporting statistics in the hunting literature could change his mind: the more powder and shot the better. He also had definite thoughts about how and when things should be done in the shooting field, which resulted in minor (but entirely forgivable) inconveniences from time to time.

Cyril, Myra, and I made our first trip to Argentina in 1983, at the invitation of Don Federico. The two cattle ranches that his family owned in the pampas of Buenos Aires province offered an array of shooting opportunities, but were superb for waterfowl. Both Estancia Cardal and Estancia Deslinde had extensive marshes, surrounded by pastures and cropland, so both water and ample feed were available for ducks, geese, and swans. In addition, Don Federico's neighbors were all close friends and readily shared their properties on a regular basi$ for different kinds of sport.

We were pleased to learn that none of the locals shot the beautiful Black-necked Swan (*Cygnus melanocorypha*) or the Coscoroba Swan (*Coscoroba coscoroba*), nor were they much inclined to hunt the numerous Upland Goose (*Chloephaga picta*) or Ashy-headed Goose (*Chloephaga poliocephala*). They considered the real sport to be abundant ducks that frequented this area in the austral winter (our summer months). We concurred with this choice and this assessment of challenge. For the reader not familiar with common South American ducks, the following is a tabulation of species we pursued in this inland marsh habitat:

Chiloe (Southern) Widgeon	*Anas sibilatrix*
Yellow-billed (Brown) Pintail	*Anas georgica*
Speckled Teal	*Anas flavirostris*
Silver Teal	*Anas versicolor*
Cinnamon Teal	*Anas cyanoptera*
Red Shoveler	*Anas platalea*
Rosy-billed Pochard	*Netta peposaca*

Chiloe Widgeon closely resemble American Widgeon in flight, but are patterned differently. Yellow-billed Pintail have the appearance and flight characteristics of female Northern Pintail and are quite common in Argentina, as are the rather drab Speckled Teal. The diminutive Silver Teal is quite elegant, with its extensive black cap bordered white below on the cheek, a pale blue bill, and prominent spots on its underparts. Although the Cinnamon Teal population in Argentina is disjunct from Cinnamon Teal found in western North America, it is otherwise identical. Red Shoveler superficially resemble Northern Shoveler, but feature bright rufous underparts, boldly spotted, and lack the green head of their male northern cousins. Rosy-billed Pochard are large and quite spectacular. Males in flight have a boldly distinctive black and white pattern and a shockingly bright rosy bill, obvious at considerable distance. A rubbery, soft knob of the same bright pinkish red develops at the base of the bill on mature males.

Also prominent in the marshes and pastures of this region are the bizarre Southern Screamer (*Chauna torquata*), a primitive form of waterfowl. These remarkable birds are at least as large as turkeys, with huge but unwebbed feet for walking in the marsh—calling to mind perhaps a pudgy, long-legged goose with a bill shaped like a turkey's beak. They are gregarious and blatantly noisy, befitting their common name. The three species of screamers in South America are not considered game birds, understandable in view of their slow and cumbersome flight.

Our first exposure to duck hunting à la Don Federico was never to be forgotten. We had enjoyed a casual day touring the ranch and visiting his friends, including Prince Charles Radziwill of prewar Polish royalty, who was then living in Argentina. About midafternoon we were advised that a "go at the ducks" was in order, so we donned our waders and were delivered to the dropoff point at the edge of the marsh. Here we were told simply to wade into the reeds, spacing ourselves far enough apart for safety. There were no blinds of any sort. Water came only to our knees, but the reeds were essentially head high.

As we took our respective shooting positions, we stirred up several small groups of ducks and perhaps a dozen magnificent swans. A few casual shots were fired with equally casual results: Three or four ducks fell, at the most. As it was a still and sunny day, those birds alarmed by our invasion settled back into the extensive marsh, joining a host of comrades feeding and relaxing in undisturbed stupor. Past experience had taught me that waterfowl are disinclined to move when in such pleasant circumstances, which made me doubt that we would fire another shot until near sunset, when there would likely be some marginal activity in or out of the marsh. About fifteen minutes passed in a manner that confirmed my assessment. Silence was interrupted only by background vocalizations of feeding ducks and occasional raucous complaints from Southern Screamer and coots, who seem to need no excuse to sound off.

We had not counted on Federico's surprise tactics. From the opposite side of the marsh suddenly came a deployment of about ten mounted gauchos waving and shouting as if driving a herd of cattle. In an abrupt instant the sky was filled with hundreds, perhaps thousands, of alarmed waterfowl that milled and circled in random directions. Confusion reigned, for ducks and shooters alike. Wads of teal would almost collide with mixed flights of pintails and widgeon. An occasional Rosy-billed Pochard added color to the scene. None of the birds seemed anxious to leave their previously happy marsh, so the shooting continued

at a feverish pace for forty-five minutes or so, until casualties finally persuaded the larger concentrations to evacuate the area.

During the height of this melee, I had the disturbing thought that recovery of downed birds would be almost hopeless, given the reedy cover and the impossibility of re-membering even approximately where ducks had fallen. But Don Federico had admonished us in advance that we should not concern ourselves with retrieval, so we dutifully followed instructions. When this spectacle finally reached its conclusion, our now silent cadre of gauchos moved into our sector of the marsh and proceeded to comb the area for downed birds, joined by the two labs that we had seen earlier in the day. Apparently, visibility was quite good from their elevated position on horseback, for our drivers turned out to be equally effective at recovery, assisted as they were by the dogs. It was a satisfactory conclusion to a most spectacular

shoot and our first exposure to driven ducks. Don Federico enjoyed our amazement as much as he did the shooting.

We were subsequently entertained on other ranches with a variety of opportunities to shoot ducks in moderate numbers, but never by using blinds, decoys, and calls, hunting early in the morning, or otherwise employing standard North American practices. Evidently, ducks are so abundant here that none of the usual inconveniences and planning we associate with waterfowling are considered necessary—at least by Don Federico and his neighbors. Cyril and I had a few ideas of our own that we desperately wanted to try, but gentle hints about new techniques fell on deaf ears. As mentioned earlier, our host was not receptive to deviation from the plan, nor was his inflexible nature open to change of approach. Obviously, we respected his position as the 800-pound gorilla and left well enough alone. Our big chance came a few years later.

We received another invitation from Federico to return during the austral winter of July 1986. On this occasion, we were invited to stay for a week or so, during which period we could enjoy a variety of sports, with the understanding that he would have to leave us on our own at least once because of business commitments in Buenos Aires. Since we had a truck at our disposal and a general familiarity with his two *estancias*, this prospect delighted us. Now was the opportunity to test a different approach. Our plan was based on what we had carefully observed: the feeding pattern of Yellow-billed Pintails. This species abounded in the marshes, but regularly left to feed in nearby cropland about midmorning. We had seen flight after flight passing in the same line over a pasture en route to fields of grain stubble. The pasture afforded little in the way of cover—a few scattered bushes—but a large herd of cattle was grazing there, which we hoped would help cover our presence.

As things turned out, cover was not much of a problem. Seemingly endless flights to and from the marsh passed overhead at a perfect height: about thirty yards up, challenging but within range. For some unknown reason, our bovine friends, particularly the bulls, did not desert us, which allowed us to use them as moving blinds. I must shamefully admit that we were guilty of unsportsmanlike conduct, and shot considerably more birds than could possibly be justified. At the time, we rationalized our greed by concluding (correctly) that opportunities like this are rare, and that Don Federico would be unlikely to concede that any different approach was worth trying, regardless of our success. At any rate, we disgracefully "pigged out." On no occasion, before or since, have I been able to duplicate these high, passing shots on such splendid waterfowl. It was entirely different than decoying birds or shooting casual passing ducks in the marsh—more like shooting high pheasant in Britain. It was unbelievable sport!

When we finally realized the enormity of our sin, we were faced with a challenge of a different sort. Now came the problem of transporting our not inconsiderable bag to the truck that we had parked over a mile away because of wet conditions between our flyway pasture and the only passable roadway. Cyril and I both had duck straps, but these usually adequate devices were sadly overburdened, as was Myra's game bag. We were loath to make two trips through the intervening mud flat. Then I was struck with the imaginative (for me) idea of using our belts as "emergency" duck straps by tightening them around the collective necks of numerous pintails all oriented identically. We then set out for what proved to be a torturous ordeal, dragging our ducks most of the way. It was only proper that we should have been punished in some way for our gluttony.

There was an amusing sequel, however. Shortly after we returned to the ranch headquarters, we were greeted by the ranch foreman, who was notably impressed with the success of the gringo method. We had determined that it would be diplomatically wise to refrain from relating details to our host; but, when Don Federico arrived back at the ranch around dark, the foreman filled him in, with dramatic reference to the truckload of ducks brought in by the *norteamericanos*. Federico, ever gracious, was as pleased as he was surprised. Upon questioning us further, his only negative comment ran along the lines of, "It sounds like too much work." We all agreed privately that we would accept this kind of work anytime.

It is time now to turn from waterfowl to tinamous. During our first visit to Argentina in 1983, Don Federico introduced us to the "partridge of the pampas." As a result of extensive reading about the history of wingshooting around the world, Cyril had often spoken to me about how European settlers of Argentina had shot native partridge at numerous locations, but particularly in the vast pampas grasslands. These accounts left me puzzled, for my amateur study of ornithological taxonomy had indicated that South America, despite its richness of individual species, was poorly represented by gallinaceous birds, except for the family *Cracidae* (guans, chachalacas, and curassows), which could hardly be defined as game birds. It is true that the order *Galliformes* contains certain South American quail species, but these birds are usually Wood Quails found in dense habitat certainly not suited for sport. Nothing taxonomically or morphologically similar to partridge of the Old World are found as native birds in Argentina.

We are, nonetheless, presented with both historical and current accounts of shooting various types of partridge in Argentina, Uruguay, and Paraguay. It finally became apparent to me, after a bit of reading, that the birds in question were actually members of the family *Tinamidae* (tinamous) of the order *Tinamiformes*, which are considered to be among the most ancient of extant families and not related in any direct way to the family *Phasianidae* (pheasant, grouse, quail, and turkey). It is, however, understandable how the confusion arose and has been sustained in current sporting literature: Tinamous have strong (but superficial) resemblance to *gallinaceous* birds and often flush from the ground in a similar, but less explosive, manner. Here the similarities end. We shall return to our ornithological lessons subsequently.

Cyril was particularly taken by early accounts of how these "partridge" were hunted around the turn of the century. Shooters strung a light cable (or heavy wire) between two widely spaced horses and dragged it across areas of low grass. The guns walked behind the cable and shot partridge as they were flushed, which shows how tightly these birds are capable of holding. We mentioned the technique to Federico when we initially met him in Houston, prior to our first trip. He was aware of the method but had never tried it himself, explaining that dogs were normally employed by today's sportsmen. Imagine our surprise, then, when he announced upon our arrival that he had arranged for us all to experiment with this historical approach. We were admonished, however, that the decline in partridge populations meant that we should limit the numbers of birds taken, to which we readily agreed.

As it turned out, this unusual method worked perfectly. Our horses were spaced about one hundred yards apart, and they dragged a heavy wire with weights and ribbons attached. We walked behind the wire and shot the partridge (actually *Nothura maculosa*, a tinamou commonly called Spotted Nothura) as they flushed. After about ten of these quail-sized birds, we halted the operation. Although it was most interesting to replicate this historical precedent, we did not consider the shooting particularly sporting, nor were we anxious to be guilty of overkill. On another day we walked up a different species of tinamou, *Rhynchotus rufescens*, which bears the common name Red-winged Tinamou. This species is much larger, almost the size of pheasant, and they are normally found in heavier stands of grass. When Don Federico advised us that this tinamou is even more sparsely distributed, we stopped shooting after two or three birds.

In subsequent years, Myra and I have covered almost the entire country of Argentina on bird-watching trips and have seen eight species of tinamous at various locations, and in widely varying habitat associations. The entire family consists of nearly fifty species, distributed from northern Mexico to Tierra del Fuego. In no location could they be considered abundant, nor capable of withstanding significant shooting. The reproductive rate does not even compare with gallinaceous birds, and most sportsmen familiar with the facts would not consider them suitable game birds. I must say that I cringe when I hear accounts of gringos who say that they had excellent partridge shooting in Uruguay, Paraguay, or Argentina. In this instance, I am inclined to take a conservationist position and say that great restraint—or abstinence—should be employed.

Having made this case, I must say that it was an interesting experience to turn historical description into an actual episode. It's too bad the brush of South Texas, or the absence of comparable grassland anywhere else in North America, make this dragged-chain technique unworkable on real gallinaceous birds. Besides, can you imagine the consternation of the U.S. Fish and Wildlife Service over the dragged-chain technique?

Aside from the rare privilege of being the guest of Don Federico, we have been fortunate to shoot in a variety of other settings in Argentina, including the topographically interesting stage near Córdoba in the north, where the Eared Dove (*Zenaida auriculata*) abounds. It is difficult to overstate the bird-hunting opportunities available in this marvelous country, or the pleasant reception that awaits the *norteamericano* shooter. Nowhere is there better food or a more agreeable climate, or a season that does not conflict with our own. Even the wine is exceptional.

The Last Goose

The likelihood is that you have never heard of Winisk, Ontario, nor should you consider this oversight a failing in basic geography of North America. You may recall, however, that James Bay extends south like a narrow beaver's tail between Ontario and Quebec provinces at the southern extremity of Hudson Bay. Winisk is just west of the mouth of James Bay (actually on Hudson Bay), at the point where the Winisk River discharges north into this giant body of water. Some maps show it as Wabuk Point. Other maps do not show it at all.

Why we ever thought it a good idea to go there for goose hunting is lost to my memory, but probably because someone had read an account of the place in an outdoor magazine. I do recall that we put together a group of about ten guys, who thought an adventure might result from contacting the designated Canadian outfitter and making the long trip from Houston, Texas, to Hudson Bay. It must have been for adventure, as winter goose hunting within minutes of Houston satisfies most anyone's desire for this type of wingshooting.

After a rather tortuous series of plane connections, we finally arrived at Winisk late in the day of our early departure. It was the middle of September 1980. Accommodations and food, considering the remoteness, were not as bad as might be expected. Our local Cree Indian guides were a bit surly, but not exactly hostile so long as they were sober. We had good to excellent shooting, depending on which location we drew on any given day, and most everyone enjoyed the experience. It is not my intent, however, to provide facts, figures, and results of our overall Winisk encounter. It is rather my purpose to relate the happenings of a most unusual day, one that remains etched in my memory.

Events of the early morning went true to the pattern of the previous two days. We departed our Winisk campsite in large canoes (with outboard motors) quite early in the pitch black darkness. On each of the preceding mornings, our guide David (a good Indian name) had slowed from full speed to a cautious pace about midway across the sizable bay that separated camp from our shooting areas on the opposite shore. My shooting partner, the ever observant and inquiring Cyril Adams, was beset with curiosity about this modus operandi, but he knew better than to ply David with questions. To say that David was a taciturn Indian would be the understatement of the century. I do not recall his uttering more than two dozen words during our entire stay.

Cyril had correctly surmised from David's alertness during the time of reduced speed that he was watching carefully for some obstruction, probably rocks just below the surface of the water. He had also observed that the typically choppy wave action was much reduced at this location. What he could not fathom, however, was David's invariable ability to know when to cut back the motor so that he could execute the precautionary maneuver. On this third day Cyril could stand it no longer and finally asked him what had been on his mind: "How do you know just where these rocks are located?" David's laconic response: "Rocks always been there." I loved it!

When we ultimately reached the far shore and walked some distance to where our "talkative" guide wished to deploy the diapers that we were using as decoys, we noticed that the ever changing weather conditions were shifting to angry-looking clouds. About dawn, it began to snow rather heavily, with huge flakes that looked like balls of cotton. When the abundant Snow Geese began to respond to David's call, it was quite a sight to see these giant white birds coming down through the falling snow—a first for both of us. It was almost a disgrace to shoot these birds at such close range as they were decoying, so we stopped after a couple of flights, which must have seemed rather strange to David, who nonetheless registered no change in emotion.

About this time the snow stopped and the sun came out, creating an entirely different day. We had seen ducks landing in the distant tundra and asked David if we might try walking them up. He simply shrugged his shoulders as if to say "crazy gringos." We all moved across the tundra in our waders, flushing puddle ducks from the maze of interconnected potholes: Northern Pintail, Gadwall, American Widgeon, and Green-winged Teal for

the most part. It was pleasant and rather sporty, because of range. Around noon, we arrived at a modest ridge that extended as a ring around an expansive flat, in the center of which was a concentration of some two hundred Greater Canada Geese.

They were unapproachable, since there was absolutely no cover, and they had seen us when we topped the rise. We sat down to eat the uninspiring sandwiches that constituted our lunch, while idly watching the geese feeding in the distance, probably five hundred yards away. The sun was almost warm at this hour, and we were seriously contemplating a small nap, when the strangest thing happened. One lone goose, a giant among giants, flew up from the group and completely circled their feeding area. It then made a straight line for our picnic site. My reaction, which in retrospect was rather shameful, was to grab my shotgun and prepare for the attack. When I shot the poor devil, it must have been not fifteen yards over our heads. I felt that it was drawn to this destiny by whatever karma applies to geese. I immediately regretted pulling the trigger, a feeling that was enhanced when we saw that it had a band and was obviously an old bird. It even had gray flecks on its forecrown. Later we learned from the band data that it was twelve years old.

This bizarre occurrence took on a symbolic aspect, the significance of which was beyond my understanding. But there was not a doubt in my mind that I had killed my last goose. Perhaps there resides in my psyche some love of the wildness that geese represent so well. Perhaps it is their honking at night when they first return to the Texas coast each year, making autumn official. Perhaps it is the thunderous sound of thousands of wings when they lift off from a great concentration. Anyway, something snapped in me on the tundra, and I knew my future contact with geese would be through binoculars. I confess that I like it this way.

Shortly after this "last goose" experience, we started back for our boat and noticed that David was glancing nervously (or as nervous as he was capable of looking) over his shoulder at yet another coming change in weather. By the time we launched for our return, gale-force winds were kicking up white caps on Hudson Bay. Adams was now the nervous one, for he has a terrible aversion to open water, which results from his inability to swim—not that anyone swims well in waders in frigid water. To make matters worse, our outboard suddenly became cranky and kept dying each time we got underway. With each dying of the motor, our canoe turned its side to the waves, and we took on water over the shallow freeboard. David responded with a typically laconic, "Bail." All that was available for bailing was a coffee can of usual dimensions, but Adams was capable of bailing about fifteen gallons per minute with this meager receptacle. He asked for no relief from me at all, since he was intent on insuring that we did not sink. But in due course the ancient outboard began to function as well as it was capable of performing, and we ultimately reached the far shore in a driving rain storm, with Adams still bailing frantically.

So you see, this day is not easy for me to forget. The last day for the goose was nearly the last day for us as well. Perhaps you are thinking: This guy promised God in the boat that he wouldn't shoot another goose, if he could only may it home. Not so, this resolution took place in the bright sunlight in a lazy setting. Lasting through the storm was Adams's incubus. There is no telling what he promised.

Rattlesnakes along the Way

My encounters with rattlesnakes have been as frequent and varied as any bird hunter I know. In the absence of hard data, I estimate my ranking among other hunters to be in the upper 10 percent in frequency of rattlesnake encounters. My geographic area of activity over the past fifty years has been replete with snakes. It is fortunate, therefore, that snakes do not terrify me; in fact, they have always interested me. I like snakes. Dr. Raymond L. Ditmars, the great herpetologist, was one of my childhood heroes. His excellent book, *Snakes of the World*, was first published in 1931 (the year of my birth), and I must have obtained and read a copy around 1942. I also read his biography, by L. N. Wood, when I was a lad of thirteen. My brother Bill and I captured any number of snakes and other critters as an expected part of growing up in the Panhandle of Texas. Somehow conventional attitudes about snakes never penetrated my psyche.

I do, however, respect snakes. I am well aware of the damage that can be inflicted by venomous snakes; but all snakes, particularly rattlesnakes, are more a matter of interest to me than an issue of concern. Moreover, their aggressiveness has been grossly exaggerated in most accounts. I concede that scientific interest has not prevented me from dispatching dozens of rattlesnakes when I have been startled in the field, especially when carrying in my hands a weapon of such ready effectiveness as a shotgun. If this reaction seems inconsistent, you will be happy to know that in recent years I seldom go out of my way to kill a rattlesnake, unless a dog or another hunter is endangered by its presence. My attitude may sound like bravado, but it is the truth.

With this snake philosophy as background, you may find the accounts that follow either amusing or frightening, depending upon your own reptilian response threshold. Omitted are routine encounters that are common to most anyone who hunts quail in South Texas or northeastern Mexico. Even a casual quail hunter has had his share of exposure to "daddy-no-shoulders." Strangely enough, there were only two occasions when I really felt threatened by a rattlesnake. Even then, each experience was more a matter of setting and surprise than actual danger, in all likelihood.

The first of these close calls was a bit nerve-wracking because of the duration of the event—or at least the seeming duration. Cyril Adams and I were hunting White-winged Dove in Mexico, accompanied by our wives and several other couples. It was late August or early September, not normally a time when *los cascabeles* (the colloquial term for rattlesnakes in northern Mexico) are a concern because of extremely hot daytime temperatures. We had found a wonderful spot to shoot along a major irrigation canal, but we were seven or eight miles from Rancho Amigos. Naturally, roads (tracks actually) in this locale were barely negotiable in dry conditions, and rain was threatening for most of the late afternoon. As the sky continued to darken, all of the other shooters prudently headed for home, but we four felt compelled to stay because the flights of dove were spectacular. Besides, Cyril's Wagoneer was a great mud vehicle, and we had the added advantage of a reliable winch on the front end.

Our decision was poor, for we were caught, not in a casual rain shower but in a major thunderstorm. It poured. In fact, it rained all night, some eight inches before morning. Such storms are not uncommon in Tamaulipas at this season. We had the choice of spending the night in the car or attempting to make it home; the latter alternative seemed marginally better because of the prospects, however thin, of margaritas, something to eat, and a dry bed … if we made it. Besides, Cyril was a fine wheel man, and I was well experienced in handling the winch when we got stuck, which was frequently the case as it turned out.

For most of the route, we could tie our winch line to a fence post and pull ourselves out, then slip and slide ahead until the next impassable stretch. It was a bit exhausting for me, because I spent most of the time running along with the line over my shoulder trying to keep up with the vehicle for as long as we were making progress. Stopping unnecessarily was not good. I was soaked and covered with mud from head to foot.

It was night when we became mired where no fence paralleled the track. Not to worry: There were mesquite trees aplenty, and our winch line was about 150 feet in length. This meant I had to get down on my belly and slide through the mud and rain under overhanging limbs in order to secure our line to the trunk of convenient trees. You can guess what happened next. As I was about to reach out for the trunk, I heard that familiar buzzing rattle, much closer to my head than I had ever wanted to hear it. Fortunately, my inclination was to freeze in place, face down in the mud. After the initial shock, I realized this was no time for fast movements, so I waited … and waited, not knowing the exact location of Señor Cascabel. I certainly did not want to aggravate this snake any further. It had already been forced out of its erstwhile happy home by rainwater. Finally it buzzed again. I determined its approximate location as about eighteen inches forward and to the right. Because it was almost totally dark, except for the distant car headlights, I had to rely entirely upon my hearing, which even then was not very good.

Leaving His Nastiness as undisturbed as possible, I undertook a very gradual slithering retreat. Maybe it thought I was just another big snake, or more likely it wasn't in the humor to strike. Whatever the reason, I was grateful. After exiting this scene with the winch line still over my shoulder, I was greeted with an irritable, "What's wrong with that tree," by the dry and clean Mr. Adams. When I explained who owned this particular mesquite, his response, ever typical of his understated manner, was, "Well, that's OK, there's another tree just down the way." He later conceded that he did know several shooters whose adrenaline would have enabled them to jerk the vehicle out of the mud with their bare hands after such an encounter. My knees were a little too shaky at that point for any such heroics. Incidentally, we finally made it back to Rancho Amigos around 3 A.M.

We shall return to other amusing *cascabel* experiences in Tamaulipas, but first I will relate my second apparent close call, this time in the desert southwest. It was my good fortune to hunt Gambel's Quail with my friend Herb Bool on several occasions. I have never fully understood how to gain permission to shoot on portions of the Indian lands south of Phoenix, but Herb has been doing so since childhood and knows this marvelous desert habitat exceedingly well. We were usually successful in finding an adequate numbers of birds, in part because Herb Bool could walk my legs off. The greatest challenge was keeping him roughly in sight, because it is easy to become disoriented and hopelessly lost in the desert, particularly on a overcast day.

Gambel's Quail have a remarkable ability to evaporate into the desert after a flush. Chasing down singles would seem to be straightforward, but it proves to be demanding work. It is also easy to become separated from a hunting partner when chasing singles. On the day of the rattlesnake incident, I was on my own, having temporarily lost Herb while in hot pursuit of quail. I had seen three or four birds flush and then turn down a shallow dry ravine, which are called *arroyos* in Mexico and in the desert southwest. The side slopes of this particular *arroyo* were steep, and lined with horizontal ledges of sedimentary rock. I had my eyes glued on where the quail had flown, and then saw two birds running down the *arroyo*. As I scrambled down the nearly vertical side, trying to keep the birds in sight more than watching my descent, I suddenly became aware that I had placed my hand not six inches from a rattlesnake. It was coiled and looking me right in the face, for it was now level with my head.

On this occasion, I honestly believe I responded faster than my reptilian friend, though it certainly could have struck when I first placed my hand on the ledge. Who knows why it didn't strike. Even more curious was its failure to rattle. A positive feature of rattlesnakes is the usual warning they give of their presence. The unnerving aspect of this encounter was the shock of coming face to face at such close quarters. My quite vulnerable head was no more than a foot from the snake, which was in a trigger-ready coil. I was so impressed by my successful escape that I returned to the snake by an alternate route to make sure the encounter had really happened. The snake had not budged an inch—nice day for sunning I suppose. I showed my appreciation for not being struck by sparing its life. But this standoff also gave the quail ample time to escape. Maybe they had a deal.

On the lighter side, I have had a few snake encounters of a less sinister nature. First of all, *los cascabeles* of Tamaulipas are plenty big suckers. I recall seeing only a few small rattlesnakes over the years, but we had confrontations with at least a half dozen over eight feet. A snake this size has a head about five inches across, and will definitely command attention. On the positive side, their very size make them easier to see and avoid. The bad news about rattlesnakes in Tamaulipas is the nature of their toxicity, for it is both neurotoxic and hemotoxic. We were not aware of this unusual characteristic until reading about it a few years ago in a scientific journal. Had we known it earlier, our constant worry about a guest being struck would have concerned us even more.

As it turned out, the amusing John Butler episode was the exception that proved the rule. His middle-of-the-night encounter was (fortunately) with a quite small rattlesnake. Our sleeping porch at Rancho Amigos was on the second floor, inconveniently located with respect to the bathroom facilities on the first floor. (We later corrected this error as all our bladders weakened with age.) Moreover, the plumbing at times was more fragile than normal, especially when refilling the (static-pressure) head tank after everyone had finished his evening shower. We always requested male

guests to relieve themselves at the far edge of our extensive tiled parking area, thus saving water for more serious visits to the bathroom. This possible midnight trip across the parking area required that each man have a trusty flashlight on the table beside his bed, to light the way.

You would have to know John Butler only briefly to understand that he would forget to bring a flashlight. Despite explicit pretrip instructions, John was just not a "detail man" and forgot his light. Gear to him meant pants and a shirt, and just possibly boots. So when nature called on this particular dark night, he ventured forth bereft of artificial light. A lone gas light in the dining room was all that lit his sleepy path. Astonishingly, he negotiated the tortuous path through rocking chairs and miscellaneous tables on the outbound portion of his urgent mission—commendable for a man of his considerable 230-pound bulk. Not so on his return, for it was then that he stepped squarely upon the poor little *cascabel*, which was desperately attempting to flee this lumbering monster. When John's naked foot (yes, he was unequipped with house shoes as well) came in contact with what he correctly deduced to be a snake, all hell broke loose. Never mind that the snake lay pitifully squashed on the paving tiles; John beat a headlong retreat for the house, annihilating all obstacles in his path, which included a hammock, three chairs, and two tables. It sounded more like a hippo run amuck than a former Stanford left guard. (Or did he play left tackle when attending that fine institution?)

Naturally, the chaos on the floor below awakened everyone not comatose from margarita poisoning. As I arrived on the scene flashlight in hand, John was not entirely coherent but I was able to make out something about a large rattlesnake. When we eventually found our small, flattened friend, only eight inches in length, Butler was nonetheless certain that he had escaped death only by a miracle. The score was definitely Butler 1, *cascabel* 0.

Rigo Tovar was quick to learn that our gringo guests had certain predilections about backcountry Tamaulipas, especially if these guests were from more civilized portions of the United States, or had not before hunted in *monte* of this remoteness. For example, they were always fascinated with arrowheads and other Indian artifacts; therefore, Rigo kept a huge jar of these items in the dining area, so that our friends could take home five or six arrowheads for their children or grandchildren to admire. His remarkable ability to find arrowheads always amazed us, as did the apparent abundance of arrow points in this part of Mexico. Rigo's sharp eyes would have been a welcome addition to any expedition of paleoanthropologists.

Rattlesnake skins were another popular item, especially for some of our British guests, who have no counterpart to this particular reptilian threat in the UK. Again, Rigo brought his skills into play. Whenever he came across a particularly nice specimen, he dispatched it very carefully so as not to ruin the skin. How does one come to terms with a seven-foot *cascabel* in a such a manner as to not damage its hide? His technique was incredible, but I have numerous witnesses. Rigo would simply take a small stick, sometimes no longer than eighteen inches, and rap the snake smartly across the head. He then placed the heel of his boot gently but firmly on the back of its head to force open the mouth. It was now time for surgical removal of the fangs with a quick stroke of his ever-ready pocketknife. And voilà: He had a belligerent, but defanged and unimpaired serpent, ready for skinning. Rigo nailed these beautiful skins to a lengthy board and treated the interiors by rubbing them with salt. Later, the finished products could be treated with preservative. It is small wonder that such impressive trophies were highly valued by even the most sophisticated gringos or Brits.

I particularly remember one occasion in August when Lord Sondes and Viscount Massereene were shooting guests. It was our custom to allay the concerns of the entire party of ten shooters that rattlesnakes are NOT a problem to be reckoned with during the very hot August daytime temperatures. Rattlesnakes are ordinarily out only at night in August (snakes are generally most active when the ambient temperature is between 70 and 90 degrees Fahrenheit). No sooner had we made this proclamation on the morning of the first day when our distinguished British gentry came face to face with a *cascabel* of modest dimensions, or at least I suppose they were modest. It was difficult to determine much about the conformation of the poor beast after about a dozen or so shotgun blasts. Only later did our guests bemoan their zeal in responding, for they desperately wanted a trophy to take home. Fortunately, Rigo had at his disposal two champion skins, which were much more impressive than the snake that had been blown to smithereens (or should we say Massereenes in this case). Can you not imagine the stories that were told back in Britain about how these undamaged skins were acquired? No doubt the truth was stretched just a wee bit.

Rigo's unusual technique of only stunning these giants (I have even seen him take off his belt and use the buckle in a pinch) also made possible a unique episode for the entertainment of one group of dove hunters. After lunch one day, Rigo showed me a huge snake that he had defanged, but that was otherwise very much alive, well, and captured in a sack. While our guests were taking their usual margarita-induced nap after the noon meal, Adams and I cooked up an amusing plan. We placed the snake in a large metal milk can, of the type once used in dairies. Then we put snake and can on the front porch where we always gathered before leaving for the afternoon shoot.

As the drowsy shooters drifted downstairs to the porch, we periodically nudged the side of the can, which caused an immediate, angry and very noisy response from the snake. This quickly brought our friends back to full alertness and action. The highest jump was estimated to be three feet. Even more amusing was their frustrating inability to locate the *cascabel*. After this satisfying chicanery, I further startled the group by reaching into the can with my gloved hand to remove the seven-foot rattlesnake for their inspection. It would have been recorded as the most macho of performances had Cyril not spoiled the day by explaining its defanged condition. What a pity.

This brings us to a second "bare hands" encounter, but certainly not rehearsed. One of our long-standing hunting buddies was a prominent doctor who had an almost pathological aversion to rattlesnakes, in addition to a somewhat spotty safety record with shotguns. We were quail hunting one winter at Rancho Amigos, which is prime time for *cascabeles*. Doc was on my right as we four shooters were walking in a line to flush birds. Suddenly I spotted a large rattlesnake under a thorny bush just in front of me. When I called this matter to the attention of the group,

Doc responded immediately with a shotgun blast into the offending reptile, his natural enemy. Once I determined that the good doctor was not reloading for another assault, I approached the writhing mass, at which time I discovered that we were dealing with two snakes, one very much alive, unhurt, and disappearing into a hole beneath the bush.

Don't ask me to explain my motive, but for reasons that seemed valid at the time I grabbed this second snake by the tail to prevent its escape. Only about fifteen inches of it still protruded. I immediately realized that I was dealing with a very large and surprisingly powerful snake. Indeed, it took virtually all my strength to edge it back out of the hole. Somewhere in the process of this engagement, two thoughts crossed my mind: First, how was I to deal with the problem that would no doubt ensue once the head was free?; And second, how much corollary danger was I exposing myself to by the frenzied attention Doc was giving to this scene? I pleaded with Adams to produce a strong forked stick to pin its head (naturally not available at a moment's notice) and with Doc to restrain his anxiety to shoot. Since I was making little headway with either pathway of persuasion, and since the head was at last approaching the surface, I jumped out of harm's way and let Doc satisfy his murderous intentions.

It was a shame as it turned out, for this *cascabel* was the "mother of all rattlesnakes," at least in girth. Although it was only about six and one-half feet in length, the circumference was astounding; both my hands could not encircle it at the thickest point. Nor was its girth a matter of it just having eaten, for it was in no way distended. Naturally, the skin was ruined by the shotgun blast, but it would certainly have stretched to twenty inches at the widest point. The only happy person of the lot was Doc. I regretted the whole incident—and so did the snake.

Cyril Adams, as mentioned earlier, is a very restrained and controlled individual. But snake encounters can produce an unexpected emotional response from even the most unflappable of individuals. One day in the early 1980s, Cyril and I were hunting quail on a ranch near Pearsall, Texas. This part of the state is notorious for rattlesnakes. Perfect habitat abounds; in fact, we once had seven rattlesnake encounters in one day when entertaining guests from Colorado. They were horrified and muttered something about killing more rattlesnakes than quail. But back to Adams. On the day in question we were having brilliant success with quail just upstream from the "rattlesnake tank," so given this moniker because of the unusual numbers of snakes inhabiting the brush below the embankment that impounded runoff for this stock tank. We, however, were pursuing birds in the upstream drainage area.

Cyril had marked a single bird down some forty yards away and was making a beeline for it. I was watching from the side so that I could help mark the dead bird, almost a certainty when Adams is at the controls. A largish bush presented an obstacle, but he straddled it smartly, only to give forth then with a loud and startled yelp—followed by one of the most amazing upward and backward maneuvers I ever witnessed. Since Cyril is not particularly athletic, and since this jump would have made Carl Lewis proud, I could only assume that a rattlesnake was involved, and I was quite concerned that our collective luck (of not being bitten) had run out. It was therefore with great relief when I saw him regain his balance (and composure), then ruin the snake's whole day with a deliberate shot. It turns out that when Cyril straddled the bush, he had placed his boot down only inches from the coiled snake, which, once again, rattled but did not strike. Incidents such as this have persuaded me that rattlesnakes are not nearly as aggressive as they are reputed to be. Yet they are obviously dangerous and deserve respect.

I have noticed some people exhibit more terror than respect, however. It is remarkable how often I have seen fine shooters, who would seldom miss a reasonable flying target, so lose their composure when confronted with a rattlesnake that they will miss it repeatedly, even when it's coiled and virtually motionless. It is difficult to imagine how a snake can be missed with so perfect a weapon as a shotgun. My wife, Myra, once found herself on a rocky hill "surrounded by rattlesnakes"—one on each side of her that is, about six feet away. Her response was not to shoot but to advise me to get her out of this predicament, and damned quick. Other veteran shooters, dog handlers, and ranchers scarcely pay attention unless a person or dog is in danger. On one occasion in Mexico, I actually saw, from a distance to the side, a *cascabel* strike at Rigo's leg and miss as he turned quickly out of harm's way. He considered the incident highly amusing, and then proceeded to strike back with his trusty belt and belt buckle.

Once when we were taking a noon break from duck hunting on Matagorda Island on a cold but sunny day, we stopped at an old well site that was surrounded by open board planking, which is utilized often by drilling crews in the marsh. Ordinarily, we would be quite alert for rattlesnakes at this hotbed, but we erroneously assumed that the day was too cold for snakes. After lunch, Cyril walked over a bit to relieve himself, which aroused a rattlesnake that had obviously been sunning himself under and below the open planks, absorbing radiant heat I suppose. Cyril's reaction was to move only slightly and give the snake a urine shower. The reach of my optimal fluid arch (and my valve action) would not have made this act of contempt possible for me, I'm sure.

But I did unwittingly gain the admiration of an old dog handler, Don Albricht. While hunting quail on a ranch in South Texas near Campbellton, his "not-so-great" bird dogs had just "busted" their fourth straight covey. By this time of the morning, I was carefully marking singles, since the dogs were doing a fine job of eliminating covey rise opportunities. As I approached the spot where I had marked a bird down, a rattlesnake buzzed just to my left, evoking the usual surprise and a quick reaction blast from my trusty Boss. At the report, the single flew just ahead of me and I centered him up nicely, making a left and a right, snake and then bird. I really didn't think much of it until Don came over and shook my hand. "Feller," he said, "I seen that did twice'd before . . . but not in that order."

I have had other bird/snake experiences, but of a different sort. Once I doubled on Scaled Quail, and both birds hit down hard in a large cactus clump. While retrieving the birds, I encountered and dispatched a rattlesnake, only to discover a second snake near the second bird. It is my feeling that snakes, because of their sensitivity to vibrations, are attracted to a downed quail that flutters violently, as quail frequently do even when well struck. On another occasion, I approached a well-hit bird only to find it already in a snake's mouth. After reclaiming my bird, it occurred to me that the rattlesnake had very likely struck the fluttering quail. This ruined my resolve "to keep it for the pot." My hunting companion that day was, however, Dr. Gary Troyer, who insisted that he wanted to keep it, maintaining any poison would be inactivated by the heat of cooking. Just the same I made sure it ended up in his bag.

The above accounts probably sufficiently illustrate the top 10 percent figure mentioned earlier. But frequent exposure does catch up with one eventually. I was finally struck by a large snake. About seven years ago on the Pearsall ranch, I was hunting with Myra. We saw birds running ahead and were in hurried pursuit. As I ran straight through some "black brush," I felt a powerful whack on my left leg, about half way up my calf. It felt as though someone had struck me sharply with a rake handle—a very heavy blow. Just then I heard the rattle (after the fact) and saw the snake, which I promptly eliminated from this earth. As luck would have it, I was wearing a relatively new pair of lightweight Chippewa snake boots with high Cordura Nylon tops. I am certain proof of their effectiveness, for the fangs did not penetrate. Curiously, I had not formerly been a champion of high-top snake boots because earlier, all-leather versions were excessively heavy for a long day of walking. I had often worn shotgun leggings over the years, but really more for cactus protection than snake protection. Needless to say, this incident changed my mind, and I strongly recommend boots of this type in snake country. The power of the strike was impressive, and it did not warn me. Naughty snake.

P. S. The above incidents are all based on first-hand knowledge. One other snake story, reported to me as true, is worthy of relating. On a return business trip from New York to Houston some years ago, I was seated next to a gentleman who came aboard with crutches and a cast on his right foot and lower leg. We were apparently both tired from a long day in the Big Apple and said nothing to one another until after the first cocktail. Sometime after this, we relaxed enough to introduce ourselves and enjoy casual conversation during a second drink.

Finally, the inevitable subject of his injury was broached. He seemed a little sheepish at first, but described the following occurrence. While playing golf in Florida, he had hooked a ball into the rough and went in search of it with five iron in hand. A rattlesnake interceded and struck at his leg, but managed only to get its fangs entangled in his pant leg. Under these rather upsetting circumstances, he began to hammer the snake viciously with his weapon of choice, the five iron. It was effective; however, he also succeeded in breaking his own ankle, much to his chagrin. I thought the guy might be putting me on, but his quite detailed account ultimately convinced me of the veracity of his story. Good thing he didn't have a shotgun.

The Earl and the Peacock

Men like S. I. Morris are quite rare. S. I. is one of those uncommon men whose personal and professional reputation bears no blemishes. I have heard not a single negative word spoken of him, and yet he has been a prominent architect and civic leader in Houston for decades, in positions where detractors are difficult to avoid. He is gracious, effective, kind, energetic in a low-key way, cultured, gentle yet forceful, and forever a gentleman. He also has that most desirable characteristic of seeing the best in people and reserving any negative thoughts to himself, a trait my mother tried unsuccessfully to teach me. Naturally, he is the world's best listener. He is, for me, an unattainable role model. And such praise is a lot for an engineer to say about an architect.

S. I. also has the rare ability to enjoy a joke on himself, another sure measure of a man who is self-assured. Otherwise, I would hesitate to relate the incident of "The Earl and the Peacock."

In the early 1980s, Myra and I were invited to join about seven other couples for a driven-pheasant shoot in the south of England. The ladies were only to be observers, much to Myra's chagrin. I had only recently been exposed to driven birds—in Yorkshire—and felt particularly keen about this new challenge. We readily accepted. The rest of the shooters in the party were virgins to this form of sport, even though each was a veteran bird hunter in Texas. In an effort to avoid embarrassment about protocol, etiquette, and safety, we all did our homework by reading appropriate how-to literature. I also lectured the group about what I had learned in Yorkshire. At least we knew not to "shoot down the line," about the hazards of approaching beaters, and the meaning of starting and stopping horns.

As it turned out, we were booked at an estate that offered little in the way of difficult topography and was well suited for American guns with no previous driven-pheasant experience. Our host was the Earl of Stanstead. Our ignorance was offset by our humble attitudes. The earl was not at the estate when we arrived, nor were we domiciled on-site. His gamekeeper received us into his capable hands and briefed us on the activities of the two-day shoot. No unusual instructions were involved, save for a gentle admonition that we avoid shooting any of the earl's white pheasant, or, of course, his prized peacocks. We dutifully engaged in the ritual "drawing of the pegs" and marched off to assume our positions for the first drive. S. I.'s peg for the initial day was one position to my left.

The white pheasant worried me slightly more than it did the other shooters, for I knew that it is not easy to discern markings against an overcast sky, however conspicuous a white bird would seem to be. Of course, there would be no problem with giant peacocks. The first drive went smoothly. We were all relieved that things had gone well and that we had comported ourselves with reasonable distinction. It was a gray day at the outset, and the wind began to pick up smartly as we entered the field. By the time of the second drive, we were experiencing a virtual gale, crossing head winds of at least twenty miles per hour.

Conditions of this type are, of course, quite the norm in the UK, so there was not a moment's pause in the action. For this drive I had the last peg on the right, and S. I. was still to my left. The head wind was crossing to the left, so almost all of the birds were drifting out of range for me, but I could view the entire line as they intercepted pheasant ploughing into the wind and then "sliding" down the line—more difficult shooting than it sounds. Suddenly a giant bomber was stirred into flight by the beaters. Incredibly, it was one of the earl's treasured peacocks. Forever burned into my memory is the image of this mammoth bird, with its huge tail bent like a letter C in the crosswind, headed straight for S. I.'s station. To my horror I realized that my ever-relaxed friend was preparing himself to destroy this "super pheasant." I shouted at the top of my lungs, "No, S. I., no!" but my warning was lost in the gale. He centered it.

Several thoughts ran through my mind. Would we be asked to leave? Would we be subject to public ridicule? Would S. I.'s remorse ruin the trip for him, and indirectly for us? What would the gamekeeper say? Answers were soon apparent. When the drive was over, all the Brits knew what had happened, but they found it highly amusing—perhaps a vindication of what might be expected from Americans. The gamekeeper arrived at S. I.'s peg looking at first a bit sad, then commenting brightly, "It could have been worse; you could have missed the bloody thing." This observation really broke the ice, much to my relief.

But the grandest thing was S. I.'s composure throughout the entire affair. He was not in the least perturbed, mortified, or rattled. As a matter of fact, he seemed to enjoy the joke on himself. After all, one peacock is not the end of the world. I'm sure he would have thought nothing of buying the earl another peacock. The remainder of the day went according to form with no untoward happenings, except for the additional transgression of one white pheasant in the bag—that no one claimed.

We were to return that evening to meet the earl and have dinner at the estate, all dressed in proper attire. This affair was typically elegant, preceded by cocktails and accompanied by generous servings of claret. In the course of the evening, meanness overcame me and I offered a toast and an award: the Royal Order of the Peacock, complete with a rosette of peacock feathers that I had conspired with the gamekeeper to produce. S. I. graciously received this recognition without the slightest hint of embarrassment or misgivings. He even made an acceptance speech, citing the gamekeeper's earlier comment in the field and instructing us about the fine table qualities of roasted peacock. The earl ended up in stitches, and we all enjoyed the scene immensely.

I have reflected on this incident many times over the years. It was a powerful lesson to me. My father, also wonderfully self assured, used to say, "Never forget the Eleventh Commandment: Thou shall not take thyself too damned seriously." S. I. showed me once again that a class act cannot easily be derailed. Thanks, Mr. Role Model.

Snipe

What is your favorite game bird? Where is your favorite place to shoot? Which bird presents the most difficult target? Inquiries of this sort are evidently posed to all experienced shooters and elicit an array of responses, characterized only by inconsistency. Aside from individual preferences, there are also issues of context. For example, how can one make comparisons without taking into account wind, weather, cover, and topography? Even a favorite place can change its aspect, depending upon such variables. A shooter may prefer decoying Northern Pintails in one instance, and driven Red Grouse in another. Choosing shooting preferences is perhaps analogous to choosing a favorite painting.

I have long since given up trying to decide. Instead, I have numerous favorite birds, enjoy countless preferred locations, and find many candidates to be difficult targets under the right conditions. But having said all of this, I will report that Common Snipe (*Gallinago gallinago*) always appear near the top of my list of preferences—and who can argue that they are tough to put in the bag? It is therefore surprising to me that many American shooters think snipe are mythical creatures sought only by naive Boy Scouts on their first camping trip, equipped only with flashlight and sack. Even those who know the bird (mostly waterfowlers) seldom pursue it on any dedicated basis. If you fall into either of these categories, you are missing a treat, albeit a challenge for several reasons.

Before we explore the hunting of this splendid game bird, it may be instructive to examine its worldwide distribution and relative frequency of occurrence. Some confusion may arise from the taxonomy of the subfamily *Scolopacinae*, which includes the six species of woodcock, plus eighteen or nineteen species of snipe (depending on which authority you recognize). For the purposes of most sportsmen, however, it is the Common Snipe that commands attention. This species consists of two races: *G. gallinago gallinago* and *G. gallinago delicata*, the former widely distributed over Eurasia (wintering to Africa, southern Asia, and the Philippines), and the latter occurring in North America (wintering in the southern United States, but also as far south as northern South America). The race *delicata* was formerly known as Wilson's Snipe in America, and is so referred to in many sports books and journals. The term "Jack Snipe" was erroneously used by many early shooters here in the United States, which is a compound inaccuracy, since the Jack Snipe (*Lymnocryptes minimus*), a smaller species of snipe, actually occurs in Eurasia, wintering as far south as tropical Africa and Indonesia.

Many of the snipe species are endemic, or have limited distribution, but several (including Swinhoe's Snipe, Pintail Snipe, African Snipe, Great Snipe, and South American Snipe) have sizable ranges—though none so extensive as Common Snipe. And none of the other snipe species approaches the population of Common Snipe, one of the world's most common shorebirds (or waders, as they are usually called in Britain). Actual numbers are exceedingly difficult to estimate, but authorities place the numbers in the millions for birds breeding in North America alone. Ornithologists use the term "cosmopolitan" when describing a bird with world-wide distribution; Common Snipe are considered cosmopolitan, with the exception of the Australasian region. A sports-man, then, can safely assume that the shooting of a Common Snipe will not have significant impact on its world population, wherever it is taken. It is hardly rare or endangered.

Why, then, are snipe so seldom exploited as game birds in America? The answer is multifaceted. One reason is the blanket protection afforded all shorebirds many years ago. The shorebird gunning tradition was apparently lost, or forgotten, before snipe again became legal game. Some modern sportsmen, even waterfowlers, cannot even identify snipe. Those who can usually consider snipe incidental game, not to be deliberately pursued. In addition, snipe do not present themselves readily or easily. More often than not, its favored habitat consists of mud flats or flooded fields, suitable for probing with a sensitive and lengthy bill, but hardly an ideal surface for the ambulatory shooter. And finally, one must credit the snipe itself: a wary bird blessed with remarkable diversionary flying skills. Except in unusual circumstances, the snipe will not likely flush closer than twenty-five yards, nor can the shooter expect to react in time for a shot at forty yards. These birds are definitely not Northern Bobwhite. Snipe shooting is not sport for the faint of heart, nor for the passive shooter.

Cyril and I first discovered snipe as a game bird along the Texas coast, after reading accounts of how they were hunted by hardy enthusiasts in other parts of the country. Our friend Clive Runnells owned a ranch appropriately called Mad Island—or at least we thought ourselves mad as we attempted to find and bag the wily snipe on mud flats punctuated with grassy clumps. We soon learned that a limit for this bird was more likely to be the limit of our endurance. Nonetheless, we found them to be splendid and demanding targets in this habitat, where flushes were seldom closer than thirty-five yards. For several years thereafter we continued to shoot them occasionally, although we scarcely could have been called snipe aficionados. Curiously (or so we thought at the time) we ran across the odd bird while hunting quail in South Texas and northern Mexico, always near stock tanks or wet grassy areas. Since the season extends over several months, we never passed an opportunity to pick up a snipe or two to give us a mixed bag.

Sometime in the mid-1970s, Cyril and I were invited to shoot in central Mexico, near Pachuca. We had numerous Mexican friends whom we had met at various box-pigeon competitions in Mexico City and Guadalajara. One of them, Jorge Conde, asked us to join him to hunt Montezuma Quail (*Cyrtonyx montezumae*) in the central highlands. During the course of this pleasant venture, we stopped by an irrigated agricultural region where rice was grown in much the same manner as in Japan: small, levied tracts that abutted one another in a waffle pattern. The tracts were loaded with snipe. At long last we had an opportunity to shoot these birds at a reasonable range and in concentrated numbers. This experience hooked us. Unfortunately, several years would pass before we again located snipe in such quantities, and only once where they would hold as well.

Our transformation from casual to deadly serious snipe votaries came about in a circuitous manner. Cyril had a friend and business acquaintance in Lake Charles, Louisiana, by the name of Edley Hixson, whom we invited to shoot at Rancho

Amigos in Mexico. He was particularly keen to bring along three of his "coonass"[1] hunting buddies, who had never ventured south of the border—or much of anywhere else for that matter. At the last minute Edley was unable to make the trip, but we took Big Mike Arendt, Gilbert Arceneaux, and the irrepressible and hilarious "T-Neg" on one of our White-winged Dove shoots. It was a great experience for everyone, including our other guests, and we became instant friends with these wonderfully refreshing coonasses. Later in the year, this same triumvirate reciprocated by inviting us to shoot ducks with them in Louisiana. So it came to be that we had annual home-to-home hunting experiences, and believe me they were experiences.

Big Mike was 6 feet, 9 inches and weighed approximately 340 pounds, depending on the quantity of his last meal. Gilbert was his father-in-law, and T-Neg a colorful little coonass who was a natural comic. To be with these three free spirits was like finding oneself in the midst of a Justin Wilson dialogue. On one of our duck-hunting forays into the marsh south of Lake Charles, we noticed an above-average number of snipe and asked our hosts if we might be able to hunt them. This petition was met with mixed reactions. It seemed incredulous to them that we would seriously want to pursue such an inconsequential bird, and yet they were always anxious to be responsive to our requests. After giving this issue careful consideration, they decided to consult Jerry Derouen, a friend who was an authority on hunting in Calcasieu Parish.

[1] *I should explain that the term "coonass" is loosely (and lovingly) applied to those individuals of Creole origin who reside in the great state of Louisiana. In these days of political correctness, it might be considered bad form to use any such moniker as might imply overtones of race or national origin. Let me assure you, however, that my personal experience, gained over many long years, suggests that coonasses are damned proud of this designation, and apply it with dignity to themselves and their associates. It is the last thing that would offend a real coonass—far preferable to Cajun.*

As is so often the case when fate takes one down an unexpected pathway, our introduction to Jerry was a jackpot for all sorts of reasons. By far the most enduring is the fact that this hybrid coonass (his mother is English, so he is not certified) turned out to be a man of the highest character and integrity. In addition, he has proved, over the twenty or so years that I have been privileged to shoot with him, to be one of the most savvy bird hunters that I have encountered. It is not unusual to come across great shotgun shots or experts at hunting a particular bird—say, Northern Bobwhite—but it is exceptional to encounter someone who has an innate capacity to understand the characteristics of all game birds and how best to "come to terms" with them. Jerry is a born hunter. Upon first meeting him, I thought this exceptional capacity would be limited to the wetlands of his upbringing, but I have since learned that his insight readily adapts to new habitat and new conditions. He is, moreover, meticulously safe in the field and is a consummate sportsman, by nature rather than by conscious design. Above all else, he is a friend who may be counted upon under any circumstance.

When Jerry was asked by Mike and Gilbert how we might be able to shoot snipe as a designated quarry, he drew on his vast knowledge and powers of observation. On our next duck-hunting trip to Lake Charles, we found that one day had been reserved for snipe, with Jerry as our new host and guide. From the beginning we knew that we had struck the mother lode. Although we were all neophytes with respect to snipe-hunting techniques, there was no shortage of raw material. The flooded fields of Calcasieu Parish are the winter home of thousands of snipe. As historical perspective, the area around Franklin, Louisiana, only seventy-five miles or so to the east, is where John Julius Pringle recorded 69,087 snipe bagged to his gun between 1887 and 1896. The natural conditions that then concentrated snipe around Franklin have apparently been modified drastically by modern agriculture, but this astounding record substantiates southern Louisiana's impressive population of wintering birds.

Our early efforts to locate snipe habitat were largely based on trial and error, and on Jerry's observations of where he had seen flights of snipe. We eventually made the seminal discovery that snipe can usually be found in wet fields and mud flats where cattle are grazing or have recently grazed. Evidently, the droppings from cattle bring worms and other natural food near the surface where snipe can reach such delicacies by probing in the wet ground. We also learned that snipe favor areas where geese have been feeding and have covered the ground with their droppings. Likewise, they seem to find suitable feeding in fields that have been turned fairly recently by a disc plow. This is not to say that routine inspection, or even years of experience, will guarantee that snipe will be present in any apparently prime field. Nor is their presence explainable where "prime" conditions are nonexistent. Our very finest day, some fifteen years ago, was in wet coastal Bermuda grass pasture not recently grazed by cattle. Snipe are where you find them.

It is easy to understand, then, why access to extensive acreage is necessary to hunt snipe successfully. Fortunately, we have had such access, which is partially attributable to Jerry's long-standing ownership of the Ford Tractor dealership in Lake Charles, coupled with family ties to farming in this region and a current network of friends who are farmers. We have also scheduled our snipe shoots after duck season is over, to avoid conflicts with waterfowlers. It is relatively easy to avoid overlapping with late-season goose hunters, since they are usually interested in rice stubble, which is seldom productive for snipe.

Snipe are equally unpredictable in other ways. It is impossible for me to say, for example, whether a sunny day is preferable to an overcast day, or whether a breeze is better than stillness, though we have found generally that flighting snipe are more difficult to locate when it is sunny and still. Perhaps they feel less inclined to move in lazy, sunny weather. The unreliability of weather as a snipe-activity indicator was proven to us several years ago when Lake Charles experienced a spate of rare snow and freezing weather (it had not snowed enough to cover the ground in thirty-five years). We seriously considered not leaving our warm beds for an attempt at snipe under these bizarre circumstances, but decided it would be fun to watch the snow fall on the wetlands of Calcasieu Parish. To our utter surprise, flight after flight of snipe bombarded our shooting areas, coming down through the huge flakes of snow like snipe ghosts searching for unfrozen ground. Presumably they had moved south ahead of the storm. Our party of five reached its limit of eight birds each in a matter of an hour, and we were gifted an unforgettable experience.

My other memories of strange weather conditions are as vivid. About ten years ago, we were hunting near a crawfish farm when a dark and angry sky produced the worst of dreads: a tornado. We continued to shoot as the wind picked up; in fact, my last snipe blew about seventy yards downwind after being hit. We knew matters were not routine when flying Killdeer and Red-winged Blackbirds were blown backward. Cyril and I were far from any available cover, and from each other, but we both hung on to the base of the nearest tree.

About this time the corrugated roof of a barn came rolling by, which made us a bit uneasy. Even more impressive was the characteristic noise produced by a nearby tornado, akin to the sound of a freight train at close range. My son-in-law, Link Smith, had taken cover with Big Mike in his truck, until the wind sucked his hat out the window, which was barely cracked open. Mike and Link joined

Jerry in a culvert near their truck, but Cyril and I had no choice but to hang on to our respective pitiful trees, as if this strategy would really have had any merit should the eye pass directly over us. Fortunately, we were spared this fate, but horrific winds blew water off the fields in sheets. The wind suddenly calmed and died, leaving us all shaky but grateful to be around. In less than thirty minutes, we were again hunting snipe, but not at this location; the snipe had abandoned it, or been blown away.

Traditional wisdom has it that snipe should be approached with the wind to one's back, under the theory that the bird will flush into the wind, presenting a closer shot. While it is true that snipe will almost invariably leave a field into the wind, my personal experience lends no credence to the merit of walking downwind, because snipe can leave the ground in any direction and maneuver with blinding speed. Our best success has come from surrounding a field with about five (steady) guns. Two guns serve as blockers on the side where the birds will leave into the wind. The other guns kick up snipe and take "going-away" shots; the blockers may have high passing shots if all goes according to plan, which it usually does not. My friends always joke about my plans and how cleverly snipe avoid them, but occasionally with this method we have sensational shooting at very high birds.

This brings up the matter of range. Snipe are not large birds (marginally smaller than Mourning Dove), and they are rather fragile. To put a reasonable number of birds in the bag, long shots are a must. Moreover, it is not likely that a shooter will merely wound a bird, as might be the case for ducks or geese. A snipe is ordinarily a hit or a clean miss. My own preference is a tightly bored 12-gauge, because I have the biased notion that 12-bores, with light loads, have better patterns than 20-bores. On the other hand, I have seen some brilliant shots, like Ed Arrighi of Houston, perform quite well with a 28-bore three-quarters and full choke. Snipe can easily be brought down with No. 9 shot, if within range, but I have had better experience with No. 8s (and on occasion 8½s), which seem to retain velocity better at longer ranges. Some of our coonass friends, who think No. 6 Magnums are the smallest size of shot made and that no shotgun shell should be caught dead with brass not covering half its length, have tried these brutes on snipe, but ultimately conceded that it was futile.

A double on snipe is rare. Although one or two a year is average for me, I have seen some exceptional shooters pull off this feat with greater regularity. Frankly, there is a compelling reason to restrain from double attempts: Snipe are quite difficult to mark and find in most cover conditions. My own practice is to focus intently on the tuft of vegetation where a bird has fallen and to walk directly to the spot, even if it means passing up shots en route to the fallen bird. No bird, even quail, is more difficult to find if cover is reasonably dense, so perfect is its natural camouflage. It is extremely helpful if a shooting partner, some distance away, will also mark the bird, since his perspective will help establish distance as well as line—triangulation, so to speak.

Strange happenings do occur. My friend Barry Allison recently shot a fine double, plus an unfortunate Eastern Meadowlark that found itself in the pattern of the second snipe. Another time, when hunting with my wife in South Texas, we were confronted with an unusual winter storm that dropped temperatures to about 6 degrees Fahrenheit. As we circled a stock tank that was frozen over, I came upon a groundwater seep in heavy grass that was not solidly frozen. To my surprise, several snipe exploded from this tiny bit of wet cover. I fired quickly, a right and left, and saw that I had doubled, but I had the notion that another bird had fallen. As I approached the fallen birds, I discovered to my amazement that five snipe had dropped from the two lucky shots, having very little to do with skill.

Cyril and I have had many peripheral exposures to snipe around the globe. Our "rough shoots" in the UK have presented the odd snipe as we walked up woodcock, pheasant, partridge, and Wood Pigeon. We have had memorable days in the Outer Hebrides (Isle of Lewis), the Inner Hebrides (Isle of Mull), the Orkneys (Isle of Sanday), and in the southwest of Ireland—all of which were highlighted by snipe erupting unexpectedly. We have also had the chance to shoot snipe in Morocco and in northern India, where they were driven by beaters. Particularly successful was a large, wet, grassy basin in Morocco. Our group of six guns spaced ourselves around the circumference, while some sixty locally recruited beaters made their way through the marsh. In this case, all our shots were of high passing birds—a spectacular memory. Yet to be experienced, but high on my agenda, are driven snipe in Ireland, where I am told that shoots are highly organized and successful.

I trust that my enthusiasm for this marvelously challenging bird is apparent. Even as I write these words, I can remember the haunting sounds of snipe on their breeding grounds. From great heights, they swoop at blinding speeds downward, with a feather at the base of the tail extended outward to create an unusual whinnying tone that is one of the great wild sounds of nature, rivaling the call of the Common Loon.

I can also envision their incredible diversionary flight patterns as they leave the ground, and I can visualize a flight of twenty birds passing high overhead. I can hear the unique squawk they invariably make as they flush. This vocalization sounds remarkably similar to the noise made by rubber boots lifting up from muddy snipe habitat. An old adage of shooters is that you must first hear this sound, then wait for the snipe to defecate, before it will level out and make a reasonable shot possible. Nice, but my advice is to wait for nothing. Take this bird whenever, and as best you can. The snipe is a most worthy adversary that will tax your stamina as well as your shooting skill.

A final word: Snipe are simply delicious as a table bird. They remind me more of woodcock than any other game bird. In Europe, it is common practice to roast the bird without cleaning it, head intact. The connoisseur bites the rear third of the head to suck out the delectable brains. Because snipe feed primarily on a soft diet, they lack the usual stomach organs, atrophied by natural selection. The long gut imparts no unfavorable taste and the birds so cooked are delicious. For my part, however, I clean the birds as I would dove or quail. My wife, who is an excellent cook, often makes snipe pot pie or Chinese fried rice with snipe, both of which are superb. She also uses British recipes for roasted snipe on toast.

For those of us who are devotees, the snipe is a noble bird—wary, difficult, challenging, and delicious. To this I add a personal thanks to *Gallinago gallinago*: You have provided many a memorable day.

Bird Dogs:
A Dissenting Opinion

If I recall my history correctly, Galileo was found guilty of heresy after publishing his work on heliocentrism and was forced to disavow his belief in a revolving earth under threat of torture. In 1981 the Roman Catholic Church officially forgave him. For the views I am about to state regarding bird dogs, I will probably suffer roughly the same fate as Galileo, but it is unlikely that I will ever be forgiven by the legion of birdhunters who love their pointers and setters.

Nonetheless, here is my dissenting opinion: With rare (but notable) exceptions, I don't like bird dogs. There, it's out on the table. I grudgingly concede that setters are preferable to pointers, but barely. On the other hand, I'm not a dog hater. In a generic way I like most dogs as much as the next fellow, and a well-trained retriever delights me, whether he be a spaniel, a Labrador, or even a cur. It is a shame that the vast majority of bird dogs so offend me. But I confess it's true.

Perhaps part of the problem lies with the owners and handlers of bird dogs. Deep down inside, don't you find the owners rather tiring? Owners of retrievers are inclined to brag a bit about their canines, but they are not in the same league as those who wax eloquent about the capabilities of their bird dogs. Witness the many jokes that make the rounds about the amazing birding abilities of Old Jim or Molly. To me, humor of this sort masks a deep-seated psychological insecurity about performance of these breeds. (Scratch that last part; I don't like psychology either.)

What really sets me off about bird dogs? For one thing they are almost all a little crazy, a clear case of instinct over intelligence. And they are wild bastards.

Be honest: How many hours have you spent looking for some stupid dog that ran off chasing a deer into the next county—time that could have been spent quail hunting? Add to this their unsavory propensity for attacking skunks, javelinas, porcupines, and rattlesnakes, all of which seem to command more attention than finding dead or wounded birds. Aside from their majestic points, which I will admit are beautiful to behold, they ordinarily have minuscule attention spans. If a downed

bird is not found in the first thirty seconds, they are usually off to find (or flush) more birds.

I am the first to concede that the above complaints apply only
to some 90 percent of the bird dog population. I have been privileged to share the field with some first-class dogs. They almost
(but not quite) make me forget failings of the breed in general. A
fine dog enhances any experience with those birds that are inclined
to hold when pointed. Unfortunately, even the exceptional pointer
or setter can last only for brief periods in the normally warm conditions of South Texas. Then some fool second-rate dog is turned
loose and "busts" three or four coveys in a row.

Comic relief is provided, however, by the excuses of
bird-dog handlers and owners for the performances of their
pooches. A select few are listed:

- It's too dry and dusty today for any dog to work.
- It's too wet today for any dog to work; or (a varia-
tion) the quail just don't move when it's this damp.
- There isn't enough breeze today to pick up the scent.
- There is too much wind today—it blows away the scent.
- The quail are running something awful this year (which
seems to be every year).
- After parading straight through a covey so far away
that a shot is impossible: Jake still has some puppy in
him (Jake is four years old).
- Same deal the very next year: Old Jake (now five) is
getting downright hardheaded in his old age.
- After running through the third straight covey: Durn,
I've never seen him do *that* before.
- The birds aren't putting out the scent they used to
(amazing how quickly natural selection works).
- Jake's nose hasn't been the same since that skunk incident.
- Jake hasn't been the same since the shock collar
fried his brains.
- Jake has gotten plumb skittish since that Yankee shot

him last year (hooray for the Yankee; Jake no doubt deserved it).
- These "stink birds" (any small bird not classified as a game bird) are driving the dogs crazy (hence all the false points).
- This kind of weed (any weed will do) is masking the quail scent.
- It's too hot for the dogs to work.
- It's too cold for the dogs to work.

Isn't it strange that none of the above apply when a real bird dog is on the ground? My friend Ted Baker, who has owned several field-trial champions and who is well respected as a field-trial judge, demonstrated this point to me quite graphically one day in northern Florida. All morning we had been hunting with his "rejects," which I had considered above average. But quail were flushing an annoying distance in front of the dogs. As a guest who very much appreciated being there, I had said something inane about quail running badly this year (taken directly from the book of excuses). Ted responding by saying, "Hogwash, I'll show you this afternoon how to hold these guys."

After lunch he brought out one of his field-trial champions, complete with a huge, iridescent red collar. He also explained that we would have to be mounted on horseback for this episode, since it would be imperative to keep this dog in sight. I immediately discovered the wisdom of this precaution. His champion, who must have had some greyhound genes, sped off like shot out of a cannon, with us in galloping pursuit. Suddenly the dog twisted grotesquely in midair, and came down in a bone-rigid point. It was remarkable that he could be flying along at top speed and stop so abruptly. "Now," Baker said, "check out those birds." Sure enough, the whole covey was only inches from the dog's nose. Ted later explained that normal bird dogs pick up "foot scent" (if anything at all) but great dogs heed only "body scent," which means that the covey will be quite close. I'm sure he must know. At any rate, the demonstration was impressive, but it did leave me wondering how he could ever hunt with a dog he couldn't keep in sight.

Contrast this behavior with another dog that I held in high regard. My friend Harvey Smith came into possession of a mature setter by the name of Rosy, who, at age seven or eight, made the usually unsuccessful adjustment of becoming a house pet as well as a hunting dog. Nothing, however, seemed to bother the unflappable Rosy. In her unknown past, perhaps someone beat her unmercifully to discourage any tiny inclination to flush birds prematurely. Whatever the reason, she was the world's most cautious bird dog. Her creepy-crawler style would have resulted in immediate disqualification in any field trial, but we loved her.

Consider the following: She never worked more than twenty yards in front of the shooter; she had a great nose and rarely falsely pointed; if the birds did not hold (often the case because of her cautious style), she simply crawled after them on her belly; she would look for a dead bird for days if the shooter insisted.

None of the above was exactly stylish, but she could hunt all day, and we put a shocking number of quail in the bag. When we came across the odd covey of Scaled Quail, which is not unusual in South Texas, she knew the game perfectly. Harvey would swing wide to the right, and I to the left, leaving Rosy to follow up the center with her tentative starts and stops. We drove the "blues" crazy, and it bothered her not a smidgen that we were violating all the usual covenants about getting in front of the dog. She hunted with us for years until finally run over by the family car at age thirteen or so.

I also remember hunting with two exceptional bird dogs in the British Isles, one in the Outer Hebrides and one in Ireland. These dogs did not have the same crazy streak so typical of American pointers and setters. They ranged widely but stayed in sight and were guilty of few accidental flushes. It was particularly impressive because I never knew if the pointed bird would prove to be a woodcock, a snipe, a grouse, or a pheasant. I had never before seen snipe hold for a dog.

Other reliable bird dogs have come my way over the years, but I must still maintain that the odds are generally against finding a good one. My own experience has been about one good dog in twenty—maybe one in fifteen, to be charitable. This assertion will win me no friends—in fact, my life may be in danger—but I suspect that you nonowners out there know what I mean. God grant me a good retriever, and I will forgo bird dogs.

Outer Hebrides
and Orkneys

If your background in world geography, as taught in most American public schools, was no better than mine, then you may not have a clear notion of where the Hebrides and Orkneys are located.[1] And you are an exceptional scholar if you know their climates and landscapes. When Cyril and I first determined that shooting in the Outer Hebrides would be an interesting adventure, our mental slate of what to expect was spotlessly clean. Our decision was based solely on a single article in *Shooting Times* magazine that recounted, in a typically understated manner, experiences of a party of shooters from mainland Britain. Details were lacking. We were intrigued, and booked our first trip for November 1983.

What we learned, over the next several years, was quite a bit about the outer-island geography of Great

---

[1] *From the standpoint of global geography, the issue is further confused by two groups of sub-Antarctic islands, the South Shetlands and the South Orkneys, which apparently were named in recognition of the Scottish islands of the same name, minus the South prefix. Likewise, the New Hebrides (now Vanuatu) of the South Pacific might add to the quandary, though hardly bearing any physical resemblance to the Hebrides of this narrative.*

Britain, including a representative taste of weather conditions that might be described as a bit harsh. More significantly, we had the good fortune to meet a breed of people whose attributes cry out for a descriptive adjective more forceful than hardy. It is my contention that a populace who reach maturity in tough, often remote environments are generally blessed with compatible personal characteristics: tough, resilient, straightforward, self-reliant, and independent. Those who spend a lifetime there are quite stalwart individuals. Moreover, there seems to be scant need for psychiatrists in communities capable of withstanding everything that wind, weather, and other natural adversities can dish out. A scattering of escapees from society also seek these harsh, isolated settings to build or reconstitute their independence. The residents are invariably fascinating.

Before recounting our shooting experiences, I should first relate the geographic background of these islands and the people who inhabit them. The Outer Hebrides are located well off the west coast of Scotland, extending from 57° to about 58°.5′ north latitude, or stretching over some 130 miles. Often referred to as the Western Isles (especially by the locals), this archipelago consists of six major islands, with Barra in the extreme south, and then South Uist, Benbecula, North Uist, Harris, and finally the largest, Lewis, in the extreme north. About fifty smaller satellite islets are part of the chain, but only nine of these are inhabited. Orientation is generally in a north-south direction from Barra through North Uist, but Harris and Lewis drift off to the northeast, as if pushed in this direction by prevailing winds.

Average winter temperature is about 42 degrees Fahrenheit, rising to a balmy 55 degrees in summer, with an average annual rainfall of fifty inches. These statistics, however, do not reveal the true character of weather in the Western Isles. Formidable winds reach gale proportions an average of fifty days in the year, and I have not experienced a still day on the three occasions I visited these isles. In the few locations where they exist, stunted plants and distorted trees are mute testimony to prevalence of strong winds. Sunshine, while not exactly a rarity, is certainly ephemeral—a scant hour or so as a general rule. Because of wind and humidity, the wind chill can be dreadful, especially to those of us accustomed to gentler climes. Also characteristic are frequent (and oftentimes violent) changes in weather during the course of a single day, typical in my experience of extreme northern and southern latitudes. I soon learned to pack rain gear and multiple layers of clothing for any day in the field, regardless of time of year. Advance weather reports are a joke of unreliability, as they are for most of Scotland.

The locals, however, appear to be oblivious to these unsettling weather conditions. It is downright embarrassing to run across a rosy-cheeked youngster walking home from school with only his woolen jersey (sweater) for added warmth and with no hat, when I am only mildly comfortable in all the layers of garments, woolen caps and Barbour jackets that I can pack on my body. These people, of ancient Celtic origin, are rugged—of both spirit and body. The Gaelic language, also of Celtic origin, is still taught in schools here as a second language; and much of the normal vocabulary, including many place names and identifying markers, is pure or altered Gaelic. I had an amusing conversation with one islander, who expressed an interest in our shooting operation in Tamaulipas, Mexico. When I explained that I thought it would be a bit too hot for his liking, he proudly announced that it had once reached 80 degrees Fahrenheit on the Isle of Lewis and that he was able to stand the heat quite well. Can you imagine how he might wilt shooting White-winged Doves in August temperatures of 105 degrees Fahrenheit—with no breeze?

Archaean (or Lewisian) gneiss, one of the oldest formations known to geology, constitutes the basal material for the Outer Hebrides, with intrusions of granite in Lewis and Harris. The Shiant Islands are an exception, being volcanic in origin, which may have something to do with their attractiveness as major seabird rookeries. Topography varies from island to island; the major Isle of Lewis generally consists of rolling hills. The impermeable gneiss has contributed, over the long stretch of geological time, and during suitable climatic conditions, to the widespread formation of peat, too acid to support any great variety of vegetation. This peat is cut and then dried for fuel, which is otherwise nonexistent in any natural form. The mantle of peat softens what would otherwise be a harsh landscape, evident in exposed fashion primarily on the Isle of Harris. I should add that "peaty water," which has the hue of a lightly colored scotch whiskey, is readily drinkable throughout the Western Isles, and is acclaimed for its flavor.

The Orkney Islands, located just north of the northernmost coast of Scotland, share some characteristics with the Outer Hebrides, but have their own ambiance. This tighter grouping of islands straddles Latitude 59 degrees north latitude and is situated squarely in the North Sea, whose weather variances (and occasional violence) are well known to the world. In some ways, however, these isles are strangely more hospitable than the Outer Hebrides—at least to this casual visitor, and based on our sole exposure of one week on the Isle of Sanday in the autumn of 1988. Perhaps this feeling is attributable to a limited amount of farming that is (miraculously) accomplished here, as compared to virtually no crops in the Outer Hebrides. The topography and landscape of the Orkneys reminded me of the coastal country of northernmost Scotland, which is not to be confused with Scotland's more mountainous and rugged regions further south.

Any description of either archipelago (Outer Hebrides or Orkneys), based solely on statistical data regarding weather or topography, fails to convey the remoteness one feels when setting foot there. Most islands, by virtue of isolation by the sea, inspire such a feeling to some degree. But for those islands located in the inhospitable, colder latitudes both north and south, a palpable lonely wildness manifests itself, especially where unremitting winds blow. The friendly comforts of temperate climes are left far behind, but the stark landscapes are challenging and stimulating. I find it exhilarating.

Of our many vivid memories of the Outer Hebrides, none better speaks to this wonderful feeling of isolation, this spirit of the untamed, than a bird-watching episode on the Isle of Lewis. There is a little-known flat area on a small, out-of-the-way peninsula on Lewis that, for reasons known only to the birds who use it, is a major nesting site for three of the most villainous and ruthless of all seabirds (if such anthropomorphic adjectives can be properly applied to birds). Each is a predator species to other pelagic birds, and each would pass no predacious opportunity to savage the eggs or young of its fellow partners in crime. These "bad guys" are: the huge, Great Black-backed Gull (*Larus marinus*) with its ugly reputation; Great Skua (*Catharacta skua*), known colloquially as "Bonxie" and unquestionably the terror of the North Atlantic seas; and Parasitic Jaeger (*Stercorarius paraciticus*), known to the Brits as Artic Skua, and known to all as a master of predatory flying skills. Each species normally avoids the other, yet they come here to nest in a large mixed colony. Perhaps it is a matter of knowing thine enemies.

Myra and I sat for an hour listening to screams of warning and alarm, and watching marvelous aerial combats and maneuverings of these brutes, which were like packs of wolves in overlapping territory: no quarter given and none asked. Surely the harshness of nature could be no better exemplified. There have been a few special times and locations in my life where I have sensed that it was not appropriate for Homo sapiens to be present. A strange uneasiness gripped us as we witnessed this consummate scene of wildness. We

backed away ultimately, in awe of what we had been privileged to see. In a powerful way it was a statement of the
Outer Hebrides: remote, vivid, unforgiving, and unspoiled.

What does all of this have to do with bird hunting? Per-
haps it will lend some context to our adventures there. When
Cyril and I first stepped off the plane at the tiny airport in
Stornoway on the Isle of Lewis in November 1983, we were

met by our contact, Andy Miller-Mundy, an Englishman no
less. That may not sound unusual were it not for the fact that
the English are not highly regarded in this bastion of Celtic
Scots. But we quickly came to discover that there was nothing
usual about Andy: not his appearance, not his extraordinary
endurance, not his considerable skills, not his restrained yet
engaging personality. As a child I regularly devoured *Reader's
Digest* and always read the monthly feature entitled "The Most
Unforgettable Character I Have Met." I contend that Andy
could have qualified for "Character of the Year," had such a
recognition been the practice of the magazine.

He was one of those escapees from society alluded to
earlier in this narrative. In his case he escaped the confines
of pre-Thatcher England, when taxation and government re-
straints stifled the ambitions of bright young men who would

have become business leaders in America. The comfortable former wealth of his family had diminished significantly. Under these circumstances, he sought independence in the Western Isles, where he had come as a youth on holiday and where his family once held property. Since the Outer Hebrides offer precious little in the way of employment base, he turned at once to the sea, working on a North Sea fishing boat. Of course, this occupation is demanding, dangerous, and brutally challenging. He was ultimately accepted by his peers, despite his background, and finally captained his own boat, which was successful in the sense that he earned an honest living—and survived. His surface then, was tough as rhino hide yet beneath this exterior was the sensitivity of a gifted, self-taught artist. We later learned that his elegant bird paintings have been acclaimed at showings in leading London galleries.

Somewhere along the line, the opportunity arose for Andy to manage a shooting program at an estate called Garynahine on the Isle of Lewis. It was purchased by mainland Brits, who thought driven pheasant would be possible in the island's one significant stand of conifers (planted by the government as an experimental project). The lodge at Garynahine was acceptably pleasant, but controlled shooting was never intended to be in this wilderness. Several shooting parties did come here, and one of them reported their experience in *Shooting Times*, giving us our lead.

We immediately explained to Andy that rough shooting in this environment was much more appealing to us than driven pheasant, especially considering the dismal prospects. He was much relieved, for he expected heavy demands from American clients. He had no way of knowing our rough-hewn background in South Texas and Mexico. We had instant rapport with him. To begin with, I was delighted to learn that Andy was both a falconer and a bird-watcher. This combination of interests is not as unusual as it might seem to American shooters, who often think of bird-watchers as natural adversaries, and vice versa. Most sportsmen in Britain have at least some interest in nongame birds.

Andy, whose angular countenance and reddish hair appeared somewhat hawklike, had both a Northern Goshawk and a juvenile Golden Eagle. The goshawk was used for falconry, whereas the eagle was being trained for introduction into the wild, after an unfortunate incident had rendered it temporarily flightless at a critical time in its young life. Each bird was fascinating to see at work and in training, but this is a separate story. I will only comment that having a Golden Eagle perched on one's well-wrapped forearm, while still feeling the enormous power of its talons—like steel bands tightening as it grips for balance—is an experience not easily forgotten. For a bunny lover, it would arouse sympathy.

We were advised that our rough shooting option would, for the most part, require extensive walking in soft peaty terrain and that our quarry would be snipe and grouse. Andy's gamekeeper, a burly Scot, was said to have an excellent pointer recently acquired from the mainland. The snipe, of course, would be Common Snipe (*Gallinago gallinago*), and our old friend, Red Grouse (*Lagopus lagopus scoticus*).[2]

We were delighted with the dog work, the stimulating (if exhausting) hikes, and the quality of shooting in demanding weather. It was a new experience to approach a dog on point without knowing which species would erupt. The mind set for snipe is not the same as for grouse. On one occasion, some distance from Cyril, I came across the dog, who had pointed but had been hidden from view. Prompting the flush, I was startled that two birds burst from the scene: a woodcock and a grouse. I visualized in a flash what a stunning accomplishment this would be: a right and left on woodcock and grouse.

---

[2] *Most taxonomists agree that Red Grouse are a race of Willow Ptarmigan* (Lagopus lagopus), *but a distinct color. Dissenting taxonomists hold it to be a separate species* (Lagopus scoticus).

To my dismay I missed the woodcock with my first barrel and was so rattled that I even failed on the second—a complete wipeout. I wanted to slash my wrists as I watched both fly away in the wind. Over the years, this image has stuck with me more than any other of my memorable misses. It was particularly painful because I have a good record with Eurasian Woodcock, and, besides, Cyril and I had a long-running competition about whose lifetime woodcock bag would be the greatest. There would be other days, however.

We also had another chance to try our hand at evening duck flighting, which is a bizarre experience for Americans, who are accustomed to early morning duck hunts. It was by no means our first exposure, but conditions in the Outer Hebrides were different from mainland Britain; wind and cold were typical.

We placed ourselves alongside two small ponds that had been carefully baited and watched the last fading light in the west. The glow of my cigar was all I could see well. As is the norm for duck flighting in Britain, I had all but given up on seeing a single duck. The dark overcast sky made visibility even worse than usual, but I suddenly heard a rush of wings, unmistakably ducks. Seeing them was another thing. I had learned two lessons from past experience: I must force my eyes to pick up silhouettes against the sky; and I must reduce my lead to virtually nil, aiming at the bill, no less. Flighting ducks are much closer than perceived. Evidently my presence had been detected, but I managed to see (barely) two large ducks exiting the scene almost straight up in front. By instinct I fired twice, unable to see even the end of my barrels until flashes of fire spewed from the muzzle. Miraculously, I heard two loud splashes in the water not fifteen feet in front of me. No one on this planet could have been more surprised than I. The massive Labrador nearby brought in two handsome Mallard, dead as hammers. Perhaps the goddess Diana felt compassion about the missed opportunity for a right and left on woodcock and grouse, and granted me this memory. It certainly did not relate to skill.

We returned to the lodge. Nothing could have tasted better than the three fingers of Glenmorangie scotch that Andy presented. I could feel myself thaw as the warmth of scotch worked on one end while a peat fire worked on the other. Even Cyril had a wee nip, violating his normal aversion to alcohol.

We returned to the Outer Hebrides some two years later for a repeat performance, but on this occasion we had another surprising encounter with woodcock. It is virtually impossible to plan a shooting trip to the Western Isles that will ensure bagging a substantial number of Eurasian Woodcock (*Scolopax rusticola*). These much larger versions of American Woodcock (*Scolopax minor*) migrate in winter from Scandinavian breeding grounds to their ultimate destinations: primarily southern England and western Ireland (and to a lesser extent southern Europe). Evidently, weather in any given year dictates exactly when individual waves of migrating birds will come through an intervening area on the path of the overall grand movement.

In 1985 we hit it extremely lucky. Although weather conditions were typically variable, scattered snow flurries had, for some days, covered the ground rather generally. Andy speculated that it would be an excellent time to try for a driven woodcock shoot in the only real stand of timber on the Isle of Lewis (outside the town of Stornoway). These conifers had been planted by the government in a vain attempt to restore forest where one had presumably existed in the distant past. Part of the large experimental tract was made up of younger trees, standing five to six feet high. The locals had observed that migrating woodcock pitched into these woods, especially if snow or sleet interrupted their fall passage. Andy had recruited twelve or so young men as beaters, whose job it would be to walk slowly through the young trees in a line, tapping the snow-laden limbs with their long sticks. We three were positioned to intercept them, in a parallel line of guns. Two of us would be near the edges and the third in the center. We could repeat each of the rather short drives about three times before we ran out of woods, which meant that each could have a turn at each position, in case a preferred pattern emerged.

Unlike most of my "plans," this one of Andy's worked out perfectly, just as charted on the drawing board. Cyril and I were flabbergasted at the number of woodcock, since we had never seen more than a random bird kicked up on a pheasant drive, or singles walked up with great difficulty in Ireland. The scene was also magical, for it began to snow and sleet as our program got underway. I am confident that we saw at least fifty birds, and more likely seventy-five. This is not to say we had fifty to seventy-five shots, for these birds were flushing quite low, making forward shots almost out of the question, considering the safety of our beaters. (I shudder to think of the damage that would have been wrought by an Italian, or French, line of guns—about as many beaters as woodcock.) The end guns had some lovely passing shots, however, and even the center gun could safely take a bird behind the line. Thanks to great work by the Labradors and careful marking by both beaters and guns alike, we produced a bag of about twenty-five woodcock, plus an odd snipe or two, and even one unfortunate cock pheasant.

So it was that we had yet another illustrious Hebrides moment. Just as noteworthy were splendid woodcock meals prepared by the Garynahine cook, a young lady from South Africa (of all places). She had no work permit, but she did have a singular aptitude as a game chef. Eating roasted woodcock on toast with a complementary claret was virtually as satisfying as shooting them.

Myra and I visited the Outer Hebrides in May 1984 to bird-watch with Andy. We stayed with Andy and his wife Bridgett at their home on the Isle of Harris, and we visited all of the major islands. Each was as untamed and wonderful as the next, not to mention that we were successful in seeing Corn Crake, an endangered rail whose numbers are diminishing rapidly, as well as Water Rail and Steller's Eider (quite unusual for Britain).

Two highlights of this trip were the Great Skua/Great Black-backed Gull/Parasitic Jaeger experience previously described, and a fascinating boat trip to the Shiant Islands, where Andy scared us shitless maneuvering his boat up to rocks in heavy seas, so Myra and I could disembark to examine Atlantic Puffin and Razorbill rookeries at point-blank photographic range. We also had the chance to sample the eggs of Common Gull and Northern Lapwing, both of which were quite tasty. But please don't tell my bird-watcher friends.

Three trips to the Outer Hebrides were to be followed by a one-week experience on the Isle of Sanday in the Orkney Islands in the late fall of 1988. This Adams-Braden venture came about at the suggestion of a friend and booking agent in Yorkshire, David Patmore. David had never been to Sanday, but had word of an English chap by the name of Anthony Luke, who was available to accommodate two or three guns for rough shooting. We later learned that we were the first (and probably the last) party ever to go there to shoot with him. We flew to Aberdeen and then took a propjet to Kirkwall, which is situated on the largest island of the Orkney group. This isle inappropriately bears the name Mainland.

At this point we came face to face with a formidable logistical obstacle. The tiny airline that serviced the other islands had only very small planes—for about six passengers—and a baggage weight limit of twenty pounds per passenger. We each had duffel bags that weighed no less than eighty pounds, with our cased shotguns neatly packed inside. The agent evidenced a stern inflexibility regarding this matter, and no amount of persuasion, or willingness to pay for excess baggage, would sway her position. Rules were rules. Imagine our frustration after having traveled this far, and being so close to our ultimate destination. But years of experience dealing with bureaucratic types in Mexico were now called upon, stirring our imagination. A different approach was clearly in order. After some fifteen minutes had passed, we again engaged our adversary and asked her if the plane to Sanday was fully booked. "No," she replied, "only one other passenger." We pounced on this opening with logic that could not be refuted: Sell us four tickets instead of two, and our bags will become passengers. (The tickets were only about £20 each, round-trip.) Although seriously perplexed by this un-Scottish proposal, she had no viable grounds for objection and bought the deal, victimized by American ingenuity. It was perhaps the best £20 I ever spent, though I would have reason to doubt it later this same day.

The flight to Sanday was uneventful. During the forty-five minutes we were in the air, we passed over many small islets and a few larger islands that were inhabited, albeit barely. We pitched down on a grass runway in the absolute middle of nowhere. The "airport" consisted of the one grass runway, the remains of an air sock, and a small shack about twelve feet square, hardly qualifying as a terminal. As it turned out, the shack was really only a wind break, for it was appropriately unmanned and unequipped with any form of communication, or even wiring. As far as we could see, there was no topographic relief, only a relentless and chilling wind blowing over a sea of grass. Our expected contact was notably absent; not even a farmhouse was in sight. We sat down on our duffel bags, feeling as lonely as two lost Texans could be and wondering what to do next. As best I remember, Cyril said something along the line, "It's a fine mess you've gotten us into this time, Braden." I responded that he was as culpable as I.

Upon reconnoitering, we discovered a semipaved track some fifty yards from the terminal building—a good sign. In about thirty minutes, we saw a small and well-aged truck puttering down the track and made haste to hail it for information, assistance, and/or transport. We got all three. When we explained our situation and mentioned the name Anthony Luke, he laughed, and in thick Scottish brogue said something that made us believe that he was not surprised we were stranded. We were invited to toss our gear in the back and cram ourselves into the front seat, whereupon he volunteered to drop us off at a place where Anthony was quite likely to be found at this hour—about two o'clock in the afternoon. We were deposited at a farmhouse on the edge of a small community, where our benefactor honked loudly and called out the window for our missing contact. In a few moments a tall, handsome chap with coffee cup in hand appeared at the door and greeted the driver, who in turn presented us to Mr. Anthony Luke.

In the process of shaking hands, he commented casually that we must be the American chaps who had come to shoot, indicating that he thought we were scheduled for sometime the following week. We came to learn that time, or any sense of responsibility or urgency, meant little to Mr. Luke. Once again, we had bumped into one of those escapees from society who finds his way to remote locations. And the Isle of Sanday certainly qualifies as remote. It was easily as removed from England as Jourdanton, Texas, is from New York City. The reason for Anthony's escape happened to be of a classic sort: His wife had run away with a wealthy close friend, or something of this genre.

But in minutes we forgot any minor irritation at not having been met at "Sanday International Airport." Anthony Luke was a charming man, with sparkling black eyes that bespoke a kindly good humor and a melting smile that complemented his warm, relaxed manner. His wife-stealing friend must have been very rich, for one cannot imagine a woman who would not be captivated by his charisma. Indeed, the farmhouse where we found him was owned by a widow who exhibited great pleasure in his dropping by for afternoon coffee on most days. She even welcomed his American clients, who were quite ready for a warming cup themselves. After coffee, we were taken in his rusty old car to the only guest facility on the island, a three-story structure that featured three or four plain rooms on the third floor, with a sterile communal bathroom on the second floor (along with several rooms whose purpose we were never able to determine). The ambiance was frightfully cold, even gelid.

I had almost forgotten our purpose in coming to Sanday when Anthony suggested that we should stow our bags, remove our guns, and prepare ourselves for a little duck flighting. No urgency, of course, there was still an hour or so of daylight, and we knew that night vision would be needed for what was to follow. The three of us, plus his faithful (and huge) Labrador, piled into his ancient, tiny vehicle, which had only one fully operational door. We drove into the windswept landscape and the setting sun. In due course, we arrived at a narrow but lengthy pond and deployed ourselves at opposite ends. I had the usual low expectation that possesses me when no waterfowl are seen flying in the area. But in the fading light of dusk we were positively bombed by ducks coming into the pond, arriving at my end and departing over Cyril. Since I could "skylight" targets at close range, I had a decided advantage over Cyril, who had longer shots obscured by darkness. We blasted away, dropping ducks left and right, based on hearing the splashes and thuds as they struck the water or ground. We could not see them fall from the darkened sky.

Concerns for retrieving game have always plagued me, and duck flighting in Britain invariably raises my level of anxiety, but I should have known better. Anthony's Lab was bothered not a whit by the darkness and recovered virtually all of our ducks, which were mostly Eurasian Widgeon (*Anas penelope*) and Common Teal (*Anas crecca*), with the odd Tufted

Duck (*Aythya fuligula*) thrown in for good measure. Our bag must have totaled fifteen to twenty ducks.

We were fast approaching the end of a long day and had worked up quite an appetite. Concern now shifted from game retrieval to eating, for it was becoming increasingly apparent that Sanday had little in the way of commercial enterprises, much less any semblance of a restaurant, so far as we could tell. In his casual fashion Anthony suggested we retire to his residence for warming sustenance, starting with scotch. It is hard to imagine, and even harder to describe, where he lived: The word shack comes to mind. We entered a small, one-room structure and were greeted by a chaotic welter of paraphernalia ranging from books and magazines to a disheveled bed in the corner, one chair and a tiny table, a cooking stove roughly two feet square, rickety shelves jammed with cooking necessities, assorted pots and pans, and a minuscule sink filled with dirty dishes. "Excuse the mess," he noted cheerfully. The thought occurred to me that we might well starve to death in a week's time. As is often the case when one fears the worst, nothing could have been further from the truth, as we came to appreciate fully in the days that followed.

Even as I strain now to recall the details, I can only partially reconstruct how "Chef Luke" managed to produce such dazzling meals in such a setting. After cleaning a few ducks, we were treated that first evening to a meal that would easily have rivaled *caneton à l'orange* in a fine Paris restaurant. His masterpieces, each evening of our stay, were brought to fruition in his characteristic relaxed style. We rambled through his fascinating "library" and chatted about practical and philosophical issues while he prepared, with seemingly little effort, meals of extraordinary quality: ducks, snipe, plover, lobsters, fish, and lamb. The entrées were complemented with vegetables that he had picked up at farmhouses of friends as we went about our shooting. Wine, however, was sadly lacking, due to the remoteness of Sanday; but I recall that scotch was (for me) an acceptable substitute. I do not exaggerate when I say that I remember no single week of my travels around the world when I had better food, even allowing for ravenous appetites produced by walking all day in cold and wind.

Equally delightful for me was the discovery that Anthony was also a dedicated bird-watcher, having encyclopedic knowledge not only of resident birds of the Orkneys, but migrant species and rarities that visited there as well. Poor Cyril: His patience was once again to be tried by endless bird discussions that held little interest for him. Anthony's natural vision was as excellent as anyone I have come across in all my years in the field, making it possible for him to point out small passerines that could easily have been overlooked, even by a careful observer. One of the week's highlights for me was what I thought to be a routine sighting of a Dunnock (*Prunella modularis*), which in many parts of the UK is rather common. Anthony immediately questioned my call, however, as the so-called "Hedge Sparrow" of England is evidently of accidental occurrence in the Orkneys—causing him to return immediately to the thickets surrounding an abandoned farm building where I had seen it. When the bird mercifully reappeared, confirming my identification, I could sense that my stock had gone up considerably in his eyes.

Our days were primarily filled with shooting snipe in the marshes found throughout the island, interspersed with opportunities for shooting ducks. Snipe flush as wildly here as in any similar habitat, even though not subject to a significant amount of shooting. We visited coastal cliffs where substantial numbers of Rock Pigeon (*Columba livia*) roosted and nested on cliff faces. This bird is the feral antecedent of all the domestic pigeons that are a bane to cities of the world. We had read accounts of how they were once shot from boats maneuvering in the surf, but Anthony reminded us that they are now protected for some strange reason lost to his understanding. We restrained ourselves admirably . . . but reluctantly. We also saw several flights of Eurasian Golden Plover (*Pluvialis apricaria*), which are akin to American Golden Plover (*Pluvialis dominica*). We shot a few simply to test the table quality, which I had read was excellent in historical accounts of the days before the shooting of shorebirds was prohibited in America. We can attest that these reports are true, particularly when the plover are subjected to the magic of Anthony's culinary skills.

I feel compelled to relate a singular event that occurred during our stay, but you are implored not to repeat it to my bird-watcher friends—even though I would adamantly deny it ever happened. Besides, it was certainly unintentional. On one of our lengthy meanderings through marshy ground, I had the unusual good fortune of flushing a snipe at a reasonable distance—fifteen yards—followed by this even stranger behavior by the snipe: It flew away in a direct, unhurried manner. When I retrieved this foolish snipe, I absently noted that it was heftier than the norm, but not markedly so. That evening at Anthony's shack, as I began cleaning the day's bag of snipe, I reflected on my cooperative and plump friend. Suddenly the thought occurred to me: This guy could be Great Snipe (*Gallinago media*)—a rarity indeed. I dug the brute from the pile and examined it carefully. Sure enough, the bill was stouter and the weight noticeably greater. I rushed inside to get Anthony's opinion, which was no better than mine, for he had never seen Great Snipe, at least in hand. We poured through his bird books and found the definitive authority (imagine finding this book in a shack on the remote Isle of Sanday), which showed detailed differences in the patterning of the rectrices. Our bird was unquestionably Great Snipe. Shame on me, but hooray at the same time! In the bird-watching world, Great Snipe is a BIG DEAL. Ironically, I saw this species again on a bird-watching trip in western Kenya, near the Uganda border, in November 1989. The flush from a marshy area there was precisely the same. But I said nothing to my bird-watcher friends about how good they taste when prepared properly by a master chef.

My mental images of the Outer Hebrides and Orkneys remain to this day indelibly imprinted. From the standpoint of numbers of birds shot, we have had more success at many locales around the world—even in our backyard of South Texas. But I will always feel drawn to these enchanted isles, removed as they are from the strictures of civilization, where the brisk, cold, unremitting wind gives me unfettered pleasure. Perhaps I should become an escapee from society like my friends Andy and Anthony.

Innocents Abroad

Shooting Red Grouse in Britain has often been described as the sport of kings. When I first came across this expression in British shooting literature, my assumption was that only reigning monarchs, titled gentry, and a few fortunate guests had access to grouse moors. It would follow, then, that grouse shooting was solely the sport of nobility, rich with pageantry and tradition. From a historical perspective, there is a certain amount of truth to this conclusion, but further research led me to believe that the term was probably meant to describe the quality of the shooting itself. There seemed to be general consensus among splendid field shots in the UK that driven grouse rank at the pinnacle of shotgun sport—the *creme de la creme* of the shooting world. If these assertions were true, any shooter worth his mettle would want to experience the phenomenon. I was no exception.

Cyril and I had our first exposure to shooting in Britain in 1978; we discovered a whole new vista of experiences that begged to be explored. Thanks to superb shooting-school instruction from the likes of Alan Rose, Ken Davies, and David Olive, we graduated quickly from routine driven pheasant to more demanding challenges of high pheasant in Scotland and Yorkshire. We longed for an opportunity to try our hand at driven grouse, but were taken aback at the cost, as well as the difficulty of arranging a productive shoot with any degree of reliability.

On one occasion in Yorkshire, we were able to catch a glimpse of how sporting driven grouse would be. During a three-day booking for pheasant, we spent an off day of casual rough shooting. The gamekeeper arranged for one low-yield and poorly organized grouse drive to demonstrate this sport of kings. My most vivid recollection of our brief encounter was one bird that came streaming down the hillside, then turned for some inexplicable reason, and flew down the line of guns. It negotiated this gauntlet unscathed by at least ten shots, which we considered an impressive performance—by the grouse, not the shooters. But later that day Cyril and I each managed to "worry down" our very first Red Grouse, further whetting our appetites.

The opportunity came sooner than we expected. Our friend and booking agent, David Patmore, lived in the countryside just outside of York, so he was intimately familiar with the shooting prospects in this area. By late spring of 1982, he knew that Yorkshire would probably have a better-than-average population of grouse. He also learned that Eggleston Hall in County Durham would accept a line of guns (even Americans) for an August booking. For those of you unfamiliar with British shooting tradition, the grouse season always opens on the twelfth of August—more sacrosanct, perhaps, than Christmas Day. This large estate was owned and managed by a charming, thoroughly admirable widow, Mrs. Rosemarie Gray, who had persevered in times of difficult economic constraints after the death of her husband. I could not help but admire her determination. She not only managed the estate, but was able, in addition, to run a full-time finishing school for young ladies from age thirteen to nineteen. Part of the curriculum was French cooking, taught by a chef with cordon bleu training. Since our stay would be just before the school year began, we were destined to be benefactors of the skills of this fine chef.

We gave David the green light to book a three-day shoot for nine guns without knowing, with any certainty, that we could put together seven friends upon whose shooting skills and safety consciousness we could rely. It was a task made more difficult by cost considerations and by limitations of time available for an unknown shooting venture in the UK. Fortunately, our background as hosts at Rancho Amigos in Tamaulipas had given us a good look at a substantial number of guests who could handle a shotgun well. We drew on this list of candidates. As I reflect on it today, the very idea of a totally inexperienced line of American guns shooting driven grouse was audacious. But at least we did so with no hubris, only naiveté. As later reported in *Shooting Times*, four of the guns had never shot in Britain before, and of the remaining five, only two (Cyril and I) had any experience with driven game—hence the title to this piece, "Innocents Abroad."

Of course, all of this was lost on the seven who agreed to join us. They were Rollin King, Howard Horne, John Butler, Barrett Allison, Bob Franklin, Gene Aubrey, and my son, Stewart Braden. This group of "virgins" confidently assumed the attitude of "a bird is a bird": if driven, so much the better. *Au contraire*, Cyril and I knew the shoot would be demanding and undertook to prepare. Forthwith, we placed ourselves in the capable hands of Ken Davies at Holland and Holland shooting school, an instructor who had helped us in the past. Although I am sure Ken was amused at the prospects of nine gringos struggling to hit the red rockets of the north, under typical conditions of wind, weather, and difficult topography, he bravely accepted the assignment of preparing two of the group.

We spent hours on several different days working with him at his ingenious grouse-simulation setup at the shooting grounds. The training works as follows: Two traps are placed at the top of a rise. Some seventy yards below and away, the shooters await targets by standing behind a wooden barrier that has the essential dimensions of a grouse butt (the British term for the screen that breaks a shooter's profile). When the targets are released, they never rise more than eight feet above the natural falling contour, which presents a target quite similar to driven grouse. After becoming accustomed to this low, incoming target, the student must address two targets, and then four, or groups of two followed

rapidly by two. Ken explained to us that the shooter must start picking up grouse about seventy yards out, and try to pull the trigger at fifty yards, which will result in impact at forty yards, giving the shooter just enough time to take the second bird in front. Shooters not drilled to do so will invariably wait too long, which vastly complicates the shot, and greatly reduces the chance for a double.

He also gave us the invaluable tip that very low incoming grouse are quite easy to miss above. American shooters are used to "covering up" an incoming bird such as a dove, but very low incomers must be treated differently. He suggested that we visualize feet dangling below the bird (not actually the case, of course), and then shoot at the feet. We proved the efficacy of these points on countless clay targets,

and also became accustomed to handling the confusion of multiple approaching targets, which simulates the circumstance we would later encounter: ten or so grouse bearing down on our station (grouse butt). He also explained that Red Grouse rock from side to side as they are driven downwind to the butts. Unfortunately, this movement cannot be duplicated with clays. We next practiced the use of a loader and a pair of guns: how to turn slightly and extend the gun just fired with the left hand, while accepting the loaded gun with the right hand held vertically—all the while not banging the barrels. At the conclusion of his instruction, we felt much better prepared, if a bit apprehensive. This undertaking would definitely be a new type of shooting.

We did our best to convey all of this, plus critical safety admonitions, to our seven cohorts, but we had no means of providing clay target simulation, or the expert instruction which Ken had given to us. Ignorance is bliss; no one seemed the least concerned. We arrived at Eggleston Hall fat, dumb, and happy. At least we were properly attired, or almost so. The footwear deviated a bit from the British standard, but mercifully there were no camouflage jackets. I cannot recall that a single one of us had a true matched pair of guns. I had a Webly-Scott box lock and a Purdey side lock, which certainly lacked uniformity in weight, balance, or trigger pull.

We learned upon arrival that we would shoot on two estates: Days one and three would be on the large, neighboring Middle End Moor of the Raby Estate; the middle day would be on Mrs. Gray's Eggleston Moor. The weather on the first day (and throughout our stay) was typically windy and overcast, with occasional sunshine punctuated with mist and light rain. We drew for positions on the first drive, met our loaders, and assumed our respective butts. The drive began with the opening horn. I could feel a distinct chill run down my spine: the sport of kings, at last.

In spite of Ken Davies's excellent preparation, I could hardly believe it when the first pack of grouse came into view. Aided by a tailwind of perhaps fifteen miles per hour, they followed the contours, scarcely moving their wings and rocking slightly from side to side. I had to force myself to pull the trigger at fifty yards. Miraculously, the first grouse crumpled and crashed into the ground a scant five yards in front of my butt! I missed a second shot, but hit a bird quite well behind, with the second gun. There was no time to observe what others were doing, or even to watch my own birds fall to ground. The action was fast and furious, demanding intense concentration. I had a vague sense that I had hit some twenty grouse, with several true doubles in front, and then we heard the horn calling for us to break and unload our guns. I was actually shaking with excitement when my loader brought me back to reality with a rare compliment: "Well done, sir."

I must immodestly report that Cyril and I probably accounted for over 50 percent of the grouse picked up on our first drive. We were all a bit stunned by what had transpired, but quickly huddled to "review the bidding." Our untrained shooters were now much more receptive to a recapitulation of what Ken Davies had stressed: Shoot the first grouse well out from the butt, and take extreme care not to shoot over low incomers. We moved on to the second drive. It was largely a brilliant repeat of the first, except that our friends, all fine shots incidentally, began to comport themselves with more distinction. I was delighted to score my first double-double, albeit two in front and two behind. And so it went for each of the five or six drives on the first day. Our compatriots were gradually getting the hang of things. The headkeeper, Lindsey Woodle, proudly reported our total for day one: 176½ brace, which said volumes about the number of grouse presented, but also that this motley group of gringos could shoot.

Day two at Eggleston Moor, managed by headkeeper Harry Beadle, was just as exciting, but offered us markedly different types of shots, resulting from a more varied topography. I finally had what I thought was a more respectable double-double: three in front and one behind. Our line was evening out a bit better now, although two or three guns were still struggling. We had a respectable bag of 100½ brace, which was entirely acceptable considering the nature of the drives and the overall number of birds. The last day we returned to Raby Estate for the finale. Our finish was quite strong: 227½ brace, which broke the historical one-day record for Middle End Moor. My personal all-time achievement was two double-doubles, consisting of two in front and two in back on one drive, and then my dream of four in front, on a pack spaced well enough to get off the four shots. At the end of the day, we were all still pinching ourselves over this stunning experience and a most respectable performance: 1009 grouse picked up in three days of shooting. Although I am realistic enough to concede that a good line of British guns might have increased this total by 200 to 400 more birds, we were smug in our ignorance. The small article reporting our success in *Shooting Times* contained overtones of incredulity. We were surprised that this shoot was also referenced in the 1983 book *Grouse and Gun*, by G. L. Carlisle. Our accomplishment was listed as one of six remarkable scores in this century, although Carlisle may just have been surprised that visitors "from abroad" (as he put it) could score so well.

Several related matters concerning this experience should be chronicled. The work of the beaters, side flagmen, and gamekeepers was truly outstanding, for this talent of driving wild grouse over the guns is an art in itself. The retrievers were also exceptional; I doubt that we lost more than a half dozen birds over three days. Lest some readers are thinking that numbers of this magnitude are gluttonous and unsportsmanlike, I should remind you that grouse are part of the produce of these estates, like lamb or beef. The headkeeper must produce what he considers the proper number of grouse, taking into account the year's hatch, the number of shoots booked for the season, and the quality of the shooters. It is the job of the guns to take all reasonable opportunities presented. Had the keepers wished to reduce our bag, they could have done so in a blink, and we would have been none the wiser. I like to think that our conduct, and American enthusiasm, had something to do with the decision to afford us this once-in-a-lifetime episode.

If anything equaled the shooting itself, it was the superb performance of Mrs. Gray and her capable staff. During the day we were absorbed in the sport of kings, and her breakfast and dinner presentations were truly *fit* for kings. If memories can be rated, then our grouse shoot at Eggleston Hall deserves a 10. I can't imagine how such good fortune could have befallen innocents abroad, and Texans at that.

The Good, the Bad, & the Ugly: Defining the Sportsman

Any attempt to defend bird hunting or to define "sportsman" is a fatuity: Those who would agree with my position do not require persuasion, and those who would take strong exception are not likely to change their viewpoint. Hunting is not unlike the budget for the space program: People either support it 100 percent, or they think it a waste. There is not much gray area. The gray area, though, bears examination.

The casual observer might think it strange that I am a dedicated bird-watcher and an admitted conservationist, and at the same time an unrepentant bird hunter. But my proclivities are not unique. I have crossed paths with a surprising number of individuals who pursue my (seemingly) disparate avocations and who share my views about the compatibility of the two. In fact, birdhunting and bird-watching are more than compatible. Not only is the playing field the same, but the players are engaged in virtually the same game.

I have been exposed to a widely divergent cast of characters over the fifty-plus years that I have been actively involved in the shooting world. It is patently absurd to assume that there is an element of homogeneity that characterizes the bird hunting fraternity. The shotgun itself may be the only common denominator, and there is, even with shotguns, strong polarity as to preferences of type. If I narrow the field—say, to those shooters that crossed the portal at our Rancho Amigos operation in Mexico—a full range of attitudes, objectives, and personality types were still represented. We saw the good, the bad, and the ugly, even in that microcosm.

And what defines the good, the bad, and the ugly? There are no distinct boundaries, but we can probably agree on who is good and who is ugly. The good are true sportsmen, innate gentlemen (or ladies), and appreciative of all elements of the natural world, including the birds they shoot. The ugly are simply louts: boorish, gluttonous, insensitive to both man and beast, discourteous, and probably unsafe as well. This leaves a lot of room for those of us that are just bad. There is hope for the bad. It is even possible that the bad will one day achieve nirvana— move, that is, into the good category. The bad may be good shots, may limit their avarice within reasonable bounds, may have too much booze only on occasion, may smoke good cigars, may be consistently safe, may not be loud all of the time, may know a few good jokes, and may have necks that are not bright red. Some of the bad you and I would like; some we would not.

The good, the bad, and the ugly categories can also apply to bird-watchers and conservationists, but we would have to define their characteristics a bit differently. Such a breakdown, of course, might apply to any broad classification of humanity—say union members or corporate executives. Some people have admirable values, and personal qualities to match; others have deplorable values, and personal qualities to match.

What do these philosophical observations have to do with defining the sportsman or proving that some sportsmen are also worthy conservationists? It is time to take a hard look at the true sportsman. He is a gentleman to begin with, and I am not talking about polished fingernails or Hickey-Freeman suits. The gentlemanly qualities germane to a sportsman are innate courtesy, basic kindness, and a broad perspective. A bird-hunter sportsman must also love every aspect of his surroundings and be able to communicate with the natural world. Ecology to him means a practical understanding of how things relate on his

hunting stage. And yes, he must love and appreciate the birds that he shoots.

Most nonhunting environmentalists (and I suppose all animal rights proponents) have an insurmountable problem with killing. They assume that the very act of killing is intrinsically wrong, despite all the killing that occurs between species other than Homo sapiens. This problem lingered in my own mind for many years. I loved birds and yet I killed them, even joyously killed them. I was finally able to make some sense of this dilemma when I read *Meditations on Hunting* by José Ortega y Gasset (1883–1955), Spain's leading philosopher of the twentieth century. The following quote spoke volumes to me:

> The hunter seeks this death because it is no less than the sign of reality for the whole hunting process. To sum up, one does not hunt in order to kill; on the contrary, one kills in order to have hunted.

Yes, you say, but why must he hunt? I contend that to hunt is to know nature in its fundamental essence.

I was also impressed by a marvelous book, *The Unnatural Enemy*, by Vance Bourjaily. He directly addressed the issue of killing, which for me was encapsulated in this quote:

> My precise feeling toward the individual bird or animal I have killed, once the excitement is passed and the trophy eaten, is an absolute indifference, and I would claim, without feeling any sense of contradiction, that my feeling toward the same bird or animal, seen when I am not hunting, is an almost perfect love.

I can well imagine that these statements would be difficult for the nonhunter to understand, much less incline him toward agreement. But I submit that the true sportsman not only understands, but is in consummate agreement.

Perhaps if enough of us in the bad category pass ultimately into the good category, then the world will better appreciate the true sportsman. God help the ugly.